MY
CHILD'S
NOT
DEPRESSED
ANYMORE

TREATMENT STRATEGIES THAT WILL LAUNCH
YOUR COLLEGE STUDENT TO ACADEMIC AND
PERSONAL SUCCESS

MELISSA **LOPEZ-LARSON,** M.D.

ISBN: 978-19-5-036753-5

Published by

If you are interested in publishing through Lifestyle Entrepreneurs Press, write to: *Publishing@LifestyleEntrepreneursPress.com*

Publications or foreign rights acquisition of our catalog books. Learn More: *www.LifestyleEntrepreneursPress.com*

Printed in the USA

To my best girls.
Bedtime rituals.
Goodnight. See you tomorrow later.

Contents

The Impact of Depression on My College Student and Me

We love our children. We will do anything for them. We want to protect them from hurt and harm and see them grow up to be happy and successful adults. When they are not doing well, we are not doing well. Children are our hope, our heart, and our legacy. So, when you get a call from your child's college that he is not doing well and needs to come home, or when you get a call from a hospital, or your child himself, stating he can't make it at school, what do you do?

If your child struggled with mental health issues in the past, you may not be as surprised about your child's need to come home. However, if your child never had any mental health issues before, this could really be quite a shock. Either way, you now have your child back at home, and he is now a young adult who is struggling with depression and suicidal thoughts. He is unable to work, he's eating poorly, and is isolating himself in his room watching YouTube videos – perhaps smoking cannabis or drinking excessively. He exhibits no motivation, may not want to see a mental health professional, and appears to struggle with even simple decisions. You call around to various professionals and are struggling to find someone who will be able to see him urgently. You also are not even sure which health care professionals should be seeing your child since he is an adult, so you start asking your family and friends for some advice. You hear conflicting information from different people, and now you are just unsure of what to do next. You may be consumed by fear, frustration, shame, and hopelessness.

This is how a mom named Linda came to my office one day. Linda was a forty-eight-year-old married woman who contacted me after her nineteen-year-old son Tom returned home from school. Linda and her husband received a call from Tom's college that he was transported to an emergency room at a local hospital due to depression and suicidal thoughts. Linda was caught off-guard – her son told her he was doing well in college during their monthly phone calls. But Tom was not doing well for months. He was not attending class, he was lying in bed all day, and he was not eating or showering for days. His roommate grew considerably more worried, and when Tom told him he wanted to end his life, his roommate contacted the dorm room manager. This then led to 911 being called and Tom being transported to a local ER.

Tom was hospitalized for four days in an all-adult inpatient unit, where he started on medications for depression, anxiety, and sleep issues. His parents flew across the country to be with him and then subsequently brought him home with no clear mental health follow-up.

Linda called Tom's pediatrician, the last doctor to ever see him, and was instructed to contact a psychiatrist and was given a few names of some local providers. Unfortunately, the waitlist to get into see them was between four to six months. Even getting into a therapist was proving difficult. Tom did not seem interested in talking with anyone or leaving his bedroom, so Linda wasn't even sure she could convince him to talk with anyone. She was getting more and more upset, frustrated, and hopeless about how to get her son in the right treatment. In fact, she was not even sure who would be the right person or persons for him to see. She did not feel they could wait six months before treatment started, and what about his academic future? How was she going to figure out how to work with the college he was attending to figure out if he could go back, or even if he should go back? Do they start considering a different school all together?

Linda was at a loss and just didn't know what to do or how to help him. She felt like a failure as a mom and was worried about him hurting himself and worried, "Will he be depressed forever?" She was not even sure what she should say or how to ask her son if he was okay for fear he would feel worse.

As Linda became more and more worried and concerned, she then remembered an old friend of hers whose daughter had a similar experience, and she reached out to her friend. Her friend put her in contact with me. I worked with Linda, her husband, and her son over the course of a year to help her son get his depression treated and then helped him safely transition back into college. I walked them through the seven key steps, as described in this book, to come up with a collaborative and integrative mental health treatment plan and educational transition plan. In the end, Tom was able to heal from his depression and transition back to school. I used this effective seven-step collaborative treatment approach to help countless parents and young adults evaluate and treat their depression and make the difficult transition through young adulthood and complete college.

According to a recent research study published by Mary Duffy in the *Journal of Adolescent Health* entitled, "Trends in Mood and Anxiety Symptoms and Suicide-Related Outcomes Among U.S. Undergraduates, 2007–2018: Evidence From Two National Surveys (2019)," the rates of mental health issues in young adults in college almost doubled in the past ten years. This was a call to action for me, and what prompted my decision to get this book into the hands of parents everywhere. The mental health system can be fragmented and complicated to navigate, with long waiting times to see a professional. This is very unfortunate, as the greatest need for services is during urgent situations. Furthermore, academic institutions can also be complex systems, and many parents and students are not aware of the resources that may be available to them or how to qualify for them. The steps outlined in this book are written as a guideline for parents to help them navigate the confusing mental health system and academic institutions. I believe these steps will help guide you as a parent to find the right resources to get your child the care he deserves and provide you with the knowledge to safely transition your son or daughter back to school.

2

Adult or Adolescent –
Who Should I Call?

Before I get into who should be treating your son or daughter, let me first go into how I came to understand, work with, and treat young adults.

I was always interested in how the brain works and why humans suffer and behave the way they do in response to suffering. This curiosity about the relationship between brain and behavior led me to a career in medicine and, ultimately, to a passion for psychiatry and research. I attended the University of Cincinnati for medical school. During that time, I began my career as a clinical researcher and studied ways to utilize brain imaging to understand the pathophysiology of major mood disorders. After medical school, I completed my adult and child psychiatry training at Harvard Medical Programs in Boston. I also continued to expand on my training in psychiatric neuroimaging research and continued to study major mood disorders, neurodevelopment, and developmental disorders, in addition to substance abuse in youths and adults. I explored the impact of how brain networks develop and how neural networks can be too strong or too weak in relationship to moods, anxiety, and executive functioning. As exciting as this part of my career was, my clinical research took me away from my true passion and calling in medicine, which was helping people end their suffering.

I was spending all my time looking at brain scans, brain patterns, relationships between brain patterns and moods, and attention and thinking, but I wasn't helping people in the moment. I missed sitting with people, identifying a problem, and helping them find solutions. I also started to recognize that despite all the great research being done, not a lot was filtering or being translated into clinical practice. Therefore, I transitioned my career more towards private practice with the goal of utilizing my research experience in brain-based neuroscience to provide a translational approach to care. In other words, I wanted to build a clinical practice that was informed by state-of-the-art, evidence-based neuroscientific research. In coordination with this approach, I also sought to incorporate my clinical skills as an intuitive healer. You see, I was a neuroscientist at heart, but my clinical training developed my love of the "art" of medicine and sharpened my intuitive instincts as a physician. I find this part of my job the most rewarding, applying both knowledge and intuitive feelings to understanding the root cause of my patients' distress.

During my clinical training at Harvard, I had countless hours of supervision with some of the best therapists from psychodynamic therapy to cognitive behavioral and family and play therapy. Each mentor helped me to see all the ways to evaluate and heal an individual. Neither was more wrong or right than the other – they were simply different ways to evaluate and consider the patient's origins of pain and what approaches could be utilized to help them work through the underlying issues. I apply these different approaches to the assessment and treatment of individuals to get a better understanding of what the main struggles are and then hone in on therapies they are likely to connect with and find most useful.

I next chose to pursue a fellowship training in child and adolescent psychiatry. I deeply enjoyed working with children, adolescents, and their families, and I saw that I could make a great impact in their lives at a critical time in development. Children and adolescents have rapid intellectual, social, emotional, and physical development that is continually changing up through young adulthood. Therefore, when working with a younger population, even small changes can have dramatic, long-term effects years later. This is why I love working with this population. I see such amazing changes not only in the youths but also in the families I see.

My fellowship training also introduced me to the evaluation and treatment of systems. Families and school systems are examples of complex systems, both of which are important considerations when dealing with college-aged students. No one lives in a bubble, and sometimes the problems an individual encounters are due to an interplay between families, employment, and even academic institutions. One of the difficulties college-age students face is that they are still adolescents on one hand but expected to be adults on the other. From a mental health perspective, they will be seen and treated in the adult behavioral clinics, and unless the adult-trained healing professionals have additional training in this age group, they may not have the resources or know how to navigate the other complex systems that the student is involved in. They may not know how to work with parents or school systems to get the student's depression treated and get them back on track academically.

This is what happened to an individual named Charlie, who was nineteen years old, and a sophomore in college when he returned home from college struggling with depression. When he came home, he started seeing an adult psychiatrist, who was very good at managing medications; and a therapist, who utilized cognitive behavioral therapy to address maladaptive thought patterns contributing to his depression. Both the psychiatrist and the therapist worked only with adults and did not recognize the need to coordinate care with each other beyond focusing on current depressive symptoms. Charlie was treated as an adult with little to no communication with his parents. Therefore, the underlying issues that contributed to his depression, including his parents' divorce and a difficult parent-child relationship, were not addressed fully and delayed his recovery. An assessment of whether his current college was the right fit for Charlie was also not addressed. Furthermore, neither Charlie nor his parents were advised to contact the college immediately to try to withdraw Charlie or take a medical leave before the deadline to withdraw from classes passed. As he missed these key deadlines, he was not able to get incompletes for his grades or get his transcripts cleared to protect his GPA when he returned to college in the future. This not only impacted Charlie's academic records, but it also impacted his financial aid and academic scholarship.

These missteps in care and academic guidance led to a delay in treatment, a poor GPA, and a return of his depression when he returned back to college. He, again, came home shortly after restarting college, withdrew from school, and did not return to college again for another year. Charlie may have avoided his depression returning and his second college drop out if he worked with a treatment team composed of psychiatrists, psychologists, and therapists who had specific or advanced training in adolescent development and family and school-based systems.

Finally, I sought out additional training in integrative medicine at the University of Arizona. At first, I began this training with the hopes of understanding diets, supplements, and herbal products, and whether or not they were safe to combine with standard psychiatric medications. Since this information is not covered in traditional medical schools, particularly when I was in training, I felt underprepared for the ever-growing number of individuals looking for alternative or complementary approaches to mental health. I also was not sure how to address all the questions that came up about non-mainstream approaches to care.

After completion of this fellowship, I learned about a variety of alternative and complementary approaches to healing both the mind and body. In addition, I learned that it is imperative to work toward optimal health to not only heal the mind and body but also to strengthen oneself to reduce or eliminate recurrence of depression and other mental health issues. This allowed me to expand my practice toward a more integrative approach to care that was more holistic and allowed me to treat patients where they were at based on their traditions, beliefs, and needs.

My training as both an adult and child adolescent psychiatrist allows me to look at an individual in isolation and across a variety of complex systems to help evaluate and treat depression in college age students. This approach, in combination with integrative treatments, has resulted in the successful treatment and transition of young adults into college. Based on my studies and research on the needs of college students, I built my practice to bridge the gap that exists in the medical field in the area of treating young adults. I developed a systematic approach to help them transition successfully into college, adulthood, and beyond. The information provided in this book is a culmination of my work, and it will help you as a parent reduce your confusion, fears, and anxiety by providing a comprehensive guide to getting your child the treatment they need.

3

Overview of the Seven-Step Collaborative Treatment Plan

This book provides the seven key steps to developing a collaborative and holistic treatment plan to eliminating depression in your child and transitioning them safely back to school. I worked with countless teenagers and young adults, and these seven steps helped many students complete college and go on to live happy and depression-free lives.

The first step involves acknowledging that your child's depression is a symptom. This could be a symptom of a biological depression, or it could be a symptom of a medical issue, recent break up, loss of a loved one, or a stressful transition to college. In order to address the symptom, a full evaluation of the underlying causes is needed to determine the most appropriate treatment. Exploration of the biological, psychological, and social issues in the context of major developmental milestones in your child's life often helps target the root cause of the depressive symptoms.

The second step of the treatment plan includes exploring integrative treatment options for your child that are based on severity and the etiology of depression. In addition, this step requires complete understanding of what your young adult wants in regard to their treatment and allowing them to make the ultimate decisions for care. Treatment options are explored in this step and include mainstream, complementary, and alternative approaches to care that are patient centered. Also, the importance of diet, exercise, and sleep will be highlighted both as a treatment and also as a long-term self-care wellness program to improve mind-body health and resiliency to future mental health issues.

For step three, we move away from depression evaluation and treatment and focus on the educational environment from where your child came from. We will perform an educational autopsy to determine what worked and what did not work at his or her current college. We will also explore what mental health and educational resources are present at your child's current school and whether or not these will be sufficient if your child decides to return. In step four, we explore specific developmental factors that are found in young adults that could be contributing to both depression and problems in college.

Step five is where we develop a holistic and collaborative treatment plan for your child's depression. I will provide an example of a treatment plan that I have put in place for another student. These plans are integrative in nature and also include the three fundamentals of nutrition, exercise, and sleep. Similarly, in step six, we will put together a plan to return your child to his current college or find a more appropriate college to meet your child's needs. I will, again, illustrate an example of a transition plan to show you how the process of transitioning back to school will look and what to expect.

Finally, in step seven, I will discuss the role of parents in the treatment process and how they can help and hinder the process of evaluation and treatment of their child during steps one through six. This step focuses on learning how to talk to your young adult and build openness and collaboration with him without pushing him away. This step is also focused on reducing parental anxiety and how to trust the process of your child becoming an adult and letting them grow into the amazing person he or she was meant to be.

It should be noted that steps one through seven are generally done in the order of greatest need and in tandem with each other. Your child's treatment can occur over months, and even up to a year. During the required treatment period, your child's academic needs will be continually assessed, and an educational plan will be modified as needed. In addition, there will be ongoing work with parents and their child to address developmental issues, parental anxiety, communication issues, etc. that will also be done throughout the treatment process.

Regardless of the exact timing of the seven steps as described above, completion of the steps will result in effective treatment of your child's depression and a great chance for successful transition back into and completion of college. These steps will not only lead to the resolution of your child's depression, but they will also lead to your peace of mind that you were ultimately able to successfully launch your child into adulthood where he or she can be happy, grow, and prosper.

4

STEP 1:

Depression Is a Symptom

Depression can be a noun or an adjective. It can be an illness or a feeling. When someone says, "I am depressed," there could be many different meanings for the individual and for you as the parent. Often, people view depression as a major biological illness, but it can also be just a temporary mood state or a symptom of something else. Depression occurs in different settings for different people and can be fleeting, constant, waxing, and waning, etc. It is important to understand the meaning behind what depression means for your child, just as it is important to understand where it came from or its etiology. It is in knowing the meaning, causation, and nature of the depression that you can truly start treating it and put together a comprehensive plan that will be most effective in getting your child back on track for school and life success.

The first important step is to evaluate if the current depressive state is due to a true biological depression or a symptom of something else. Individuals can also have both a biological depression and symptomatic depression. For example, you can struggle with a chronic biological depression; and then, on top of that, experience grief due to a major stressor, such as a loss of a loved one, injury, or loss of a job. If treatment does not focus on both causes of depression, the chances of recovery are reduced. This can lead to worsening depression, suicidality, and delayed recovery.

This was the case for eighteen-year-old Karen, who had a history of moderate depressive episodes and then suffered the loss of a grandparent who she was very close to. Karen was distraught over the death of her grandmother, which was to be expected initially. However, over the next several weeks, her depression worsened. Family members felt her symptoms were due to the loss of her grandmother and felt her grief was normal. But, as the next few months passed, her depression continued to worsen. She struggled to get out of bed, stopped eating, and had severe suicidal thoughts that she did not share with her family. She began having visual and auditory hallucinations of seeing her grandmother in her home and eventually was hospitalized. Her recovery took over twelve months and required significant medical intervention, which was avoidable if her depression was evaluated and treated sooner.

To begin understanding the root cause of depressive symptoms, we can first start by assessing the quality, quantity, severity, and duration of symptoms. Next we can look for the presence or absence of any recent stressful events or "triggers" for the depressive symptoms. Other important factors to consider include medical issues and family history, or genetic predisposition for depression. Individuals with chronic and severe depression – depression that is consistent, lasts for several weeks, and has discrete episodes – show typical characteristics for a biological depression. The typical symptoms of depression include:

- Down or depressed mood
- Feelings of guilt or worthlessness
- Feelings of emptiness, hopelessness, or helplessness
- Low or no energy or the opposite – agitated or rest-less energy
- Low motivation
- Inability to enjoy previously enjoyed activities or loss of pleasure in most things
- Problems with sleep – either too much or too little
- Problems with appetite – either too much or too little
- Poor concentration, distractibility, and inability to make simple decisions
- Body aches and pains
- Suicidal ideation

Tom, a twenty-two-year-old male who was in his second semester of college, is an example of someone with moderate to severe biological depressive symptoms. He had low moods that started during the Christmas break, but his moods got worse after he went back to college. For the past 6 weeks, he struggled to get out of bed in the morning and go to classes. He had no energy or motivation to do his homework and had little to no appetite. He was able to shower and brush his teeth most days but had to push himself to do this, as he felt like his body was weighed down by "lead." Tom was not hanging out with friends and was unable to find enjoyment in anything. He had some suicidal thoughts and hoped he would "not wake up" in the morning but had no clear plan for how he would end his life. His roommate was worried about him, as this was a dramatic change for him from over the past two months. Tom's parents were also worried about him, and also thought this was a sudden change in behavior for him. Prior to his current depression, Tom was described as always being an upbeat person with family and peers and was highly successful in school.

In contrast to Tom, Jim's story would be a great example of depression as a trigger symptom. Jim was a twenty-two-year-old male who was in his second semester of college. He had a breakup with his girlfriend over Christmas when he came home for break. For the past 2 weeks he was down and tearful at times at school and expressed sadness over his loss of his girlfriend. He struggled to fall asleep most nights but was able to get out of bed and go to his classes. His appetite was lower, and he was eating a bit less. He was easily distracted and found it hard to concentrate on his studies, but his grades were not significantly changed. He did have some good days and enjoyed his friends, who were a good source of support for him. He denied having suicidal thoughts of any kind but was hoping his depression would go away soon, so he could "get on with his life."

Using the two examples above, we can assess the severity of depressive symptoms by looking at key areas of function, including 1) physical dysfunction with sleep, eating, and energy level; 2) motivation; 3) ability to enjoy activities; 4) social impairments; 5) work or school difficulties; and 6) presence and severity of suicidal thoughts. In the first example, Tom had moderate to severe problems with physical symptoms, such as low energy, sleeping too much, and not eating. He was isolating from friends and was unable to enjoy any activities he used to enjoy. He was not attending classes, had low motivation, and had suicidal ideation. Taken together, his symptoms pointed to a true biological depression. Now in comparison to Tom,

Jim's depressive symptoms are much less severe. He expressed depression but had few physical issues and was able to hang out with friends and enjoy their company. He was also able to attend school with minimal impact on his grades. His symptoms were mild overall and suggested his depression was not a true biological depression but more a symptom of his recent stressful breakup.

Medical Considerations for Depressive Symptoms

There are many medical causes of depression that should be ruled out before giving a diagnosis of a major depressive disorder. For instance, endocrine issues, such as low thyroid hormones, can cause depressive symptoms. In addition, immunological, rheumatological, and inflammatory illnesses and infections can also predispose someone to both depression and having depressive symptoms. Nutritional deficiencies in vitamins, such as folate, B12, and vitamin D, are also associated with depressive symptoms. Sleep apnea is also often an underdiagnosed cause for depressive symptoms. One of the confusing aspects of medical causes of depression is that certain medical issues can cause depressive symptoms; but there is also a higher risk of a biological depression in these individuals. For example, individuals with chronic medical issues, such as multiple sclerosis, cystic fibrosis, Crohn's disease, and heart problems, often have depression symptoms due to the stress of the medical illness, but the diseases or medications used to treat them can also increase risk for a true biological depression. The key here is to evaluate and ultimately treat the body and mind together to improve outcomes.

Because of the many biological causes of depressive symptoms and the higher rate of depressive symptoms in chronic medical issues, a full battery of laboratory testing and possible MRI, EEG, and sleep testing may be indicated. Some basic laboratory testing to consider includes a full blood count, metabolic panel, nutritional analyses (Vitamin D, B12, folate, Copper, magnesium, zinc), thyroid panel, lipid panel, and drug testing. Another test that may be useful includes methylenetetrahydrofolate reductase (MTHR) genetic testing to evaluate whether folate is appropriately being metabolized correctly. Blood glucose levels, hemoglobin A1c (to measure long-term blood glucose), and insulin levels can also be measured to evaluate for diabetes or metabolic syndrome. If individuals have severe fatigue, low-grade fevers, body sweats, and/or generalized body aches and pains, I also recommend labs to rule out infections like mononucleosis, Lyme disease (if you live in tick-infested areas), or HIV.

If there are any neurological symptoms or psychotic symptoms, an MRI and/or EEG may be also be considered to evaluate for multiple sclerosis, tumors, and seizures. If depressive and body symptoms are atypical or particularly severe, testing for overall body inflammation would also be useful. Elevations in inflammatory markers can suggest a possible immunological, rheumatological, or inflammatory process is occurring and requires a more extensive medical work-up by a specialist.

Some people may also be experiencing adrenal fatigue due to severe or chronic stress. Some practitioners can and will evaluate the cortisol system to assess the impact of HPA axis issues on overall mood and body health.

Finally, hormonal issues, particularly in females, can also cause depressive symptoms. Evaluation of menstrual cycles, premenstrual Syndrome (PMS) symptoms, polycystic ovarian syndrome symptoms, and possibly hormonal levels may be indicated if depressive symptoms worsen around menses or is associated with severe cramping.

It's important to work with your doctor to rule out whether or not medical issues are the cause of or are contributing to depression symptoms, as addressing the medical issues can greatly increase your ability to resolve depressive symptoms.

Personality Traits and Depressive Symptoms

Certain personality traits or specific/maladaptive coping strategies can also lead to depression or depressive symptoms. Good examples of this are individuals with a shy, anxious, or perfectionistic temperament. Anxiety or fear is the underlying feeling for these individuals, and it can be difficult for them to keep it under control. Anxiety can be exhausting mentally and physically, thereby causing people to "give up" and develop depression symptoms, such as hopelessness, fatigue, loss of interest in life, problems sleeping, and appetite issues. It can also lead to social isolation and restricted activities due to the desire to avoid situations that could trigger anxiety.

Individuals that are more rigid or have black and white think-ing are also prone to developing depression due to interpersonal struggles and pessimism that develops with an inability to see the world in shades of gray. Individuals that struggle with mood instability, poor relationship dynamics, or who struggle with trust can also struggle with symptoms of depression. These underlying traits and resulting coping strategies can lead to feelings of failure, not being good enough, and/or struggling with relationships that lead to loneliness and feeling "different" or left out. This can be particularly hard on teens and young adults who are trying to figure out who they are and find a peer group to connect with.

There is formalized testing that can be performed to get a clearer picture of temperament and coping strategies, which can aid in evaluation and treatment. However, this is not always necessary, and simply asking about temperament growing up, parental and peer relationships over childhood and adolescence, coping strategies for dealing with difficult issues, and mood stability are often enough to get a good idea of issues that could be driving some depression symptoms. Identifying specific personality traits is an important aspect of the depression evaluation, as all human traits have "good" and "bad" components to them. The key is to turn the perceived "negative" aspects of our traits to our advantage. For example, people with an anxious temperament can learn to turn that anxious energy into high levels of productivity, or a strong-willed or stubborn adolescent can turn that trait into a "never give up" attitude.

Regarding coping strategies, often individuals will utilize certain strategies that worked for them when they were younger, but then they get "stuck" using the same strategies as they get older. These immature strategies can be maladaptive, especially as you get older, and they need to be addressed so that healthy strategies can be used in their place. Some examples of immature coping strategies that adolescents can carry into adulthood include acting out behaviors, denial, projection and projective identification, and passive aggression. Others include rationalization, isolation, and intellectualization. Helping adolescents and young adults develop more mature coping strategies, such as humor and altruism; and substituting in healthy behaviors, such as good diet, exercise, and meditation, is key to the maturation process and leads to more effective job, peer, and significant other relationships.

Let's utilize Kim and Gary to illustrate these concepts more clearly. Kim is an eighteen-year-old college student who has a long history of being easily angered and had intense moods swings that she had difficulty controlling most of her life. Because of her intense moods, she overwhelmed her parents and had trouble keeping friends. In order to manage her moods, she developed acting out behaviors, such as cutting herself and alcohol misuse. As she struggled with relationships, she became mistrustful and had a fear of abandonment. She often projected these fears onto friends and family and accused them of not loving her or wanting to be her friend. Her moods, behavior, and accusations set the stage to push people away, which is exactly what she feared most. For Kim, focusing on teaching her how to manage her moods in healthy ways and helping her see how her behaviors were getting her the opposite of what she wanted helped Kim gain control of her moods and establish healthy relationships with others. Her cutting behaviors and alcohol misuse were replaced with mindfulness-based meditation, breathing exercises, and daily exercise.

In contrast to Kim, Gary was a twenty-year-old college student who was always very quiet and reserved, and often spent a lot of time alone. He was very anxious underneath his quiet façade but was not able to acknowledge his anxiety as a feeling. He would avoid situations that could cause anxiety and would manage his anxiety by using controlling behaviors, such as restricting his food intake and constantly monitoring his calories. He also was overly organized and would become very upset if his room, homework assignments, etc. were not perfectly in order. Gary would rationalize his low food intake and perfectionistic behaviors by citing his desires to be healthy, avoid obesity, and "achieve perfection." Gary's treatment focused on first getting him to acknowledge and feel his anxiety, and then he was taught skills to manage his anxiety so he could let go of his controlling behaviors. Gary was also taught healthier coping strategies, including writing down his feelings in a journal, daily exercise, and developing a healthier relationship with food.

Social Stressors and Depression

A variety of social stress, both good and bad, can also lead to depression and depressive symptoms. We all know the negative impact of "bad" stressful events, such as divorce, school failure, breakups, and financial stress. However, "good" stress affects the body in the same way. Examples include moving away to college, vacations, promotions, marriages, winning the lottery, etc. When the body detects "stress," it will release stress hormones, like cortisol, to help manage the brain and body's reaction to stress. However, when stress hormones are constantly being released due to a major stressful event or multiple smaller events, the increasing levels of these hormones can lead to depressive symptoms.

When stress, good or bad, accumulates and exceeds your capacity to cope, you will often become overwhelmed, down, and even depressed. Resilience and the ability to bounce back or cope with stress is different for everyone, but there are ways to increase your resilience. We will talk more about coping strategies in Chapter 5. For this step, it is important to assess what the current stressful life events were over the past month, year, and lifetime to assess the level of significant life events that could contribute to depressive symptoms. In addition, I also like to do an assessment of strengths and see how an individual overcame major life events in the past, as this gives me clues on how to help them figure out how to solve their struggles now.

Learning Issues and Depression

Scott was an eighteen-year-old college student who dropped out of school his first semester due to poor grades and depression. He never experienced depression in the past, and he always did well in school. On closer evaluation of his high school performance, he was noted to be "smart and charismatic" but "always a little behind." He procrastinated on his assignments, often asking for extensions from teachers, and was always the last one to complete his tests. He went to a small private high school, and there was considerable flexibility with assignments and tests, and his parents received notification if he was behind on his assignments. His parents were very involved in checking his grades and helping him stay on task and organized. Nevertheless, Scott was very bright and excelled on tests and, therefore, no one ever raised any concern he may have attention issues or had poor study and organizational skills. When he went to a large university, he quickly became overwhelmed by the quantity of assignments. No one was helping him stay organized and on task. He was too embarrassed to let his parents know of his academic struggles, and he wanted to be "independent." There was no set schedule for him to sleep, eat, or do homework, and he was not aware of how useful having a structure in place would be for him. As he fell farther and farther behind, he became overwhelmed, depressed, ashamed, and eventually gave up on school.

Believe it or not, learning issues are not always picked up or addressed in early education or even during high school. These issues are often missed in individuals with above average intellectual abilities who were able to "get by" on their smarts and used what I call "creative workarounds." However, in college and advanced education, the amount of material and the progressively harder classes can result in a student not being able to "get by" any longer. He may start to fall behind and not understand why. He can feel lazy, overwhelmed, afraid, or ashamed to ask for help and just not know what resources are available. There are also students who will be aware of some of their learning difficulties as they were previously diagnosed in early education. However, when they transition to college, they may not be able to successfully navigate the college disability services, and thus start falling behind.

One reason for the difficulty in navigating disability services is that the process to get accommodation can be confusing and time consuming, especially if a student is trying to access services after they start college, or what I call the "let's wait and see if I need it" approach. Each college and university have different requirements to obtain services, and access to some services just may not be available. Students might also feel embarrassed to ask for help or don't want to feel "different" from their peers. This can cause them to fall behind and become unable to figure out how best to catch up on their own.

When you add in learning issues with little to no independent learning skills or living structure and lack of academic support, this can be a perfect storm for impending school failure. For example, students are required to be fully independent in figuring out their own classes, homework and study schedule, and organizing projects and big assignments. They may also struggle finding tutoring or help in specific classes. This can be particularly hard for students who had significant parental guidance and involvement in their academics during high school. The sudden withdrawal of parental involvement can be a major transitional difficulty when moving from adolescence to adulthood. Again, these school issues can lead to increasing struggles in self-esteem, confidence, and bring up feelings of failure, humiliation, and depression. Therefore, any evidence of learning issues, attention issues, or cognitive dysfunction of any kind should prompt an evaluation with a neuropsychologist. A neuropsychologist is a specialized psychologist who is able to evaluate your child for the presence of a specific learning issue, such as math or reading issues, processing issues, and difficulties with certain types of memory or executive functioning. Having such an evaluation will help your student meet the requirements to obtain accommodations in college. The evaluation can identify weaknesses in learning skills and help in putting together a learning plan that focuses on the needed learning skills/strategies for your child.

Finally, not everyone with school struggles will have learning issues, but they may have just made it through high school without learning "how to study." Problems with setting a study schedule, taking breaks from studying, and learning how to take multiple choice tests are examples of strategies that can be easily taught and can make a big difference in your child's academic success. There are several ways parents can help their child get these learning strategies, such as tutoring and/or encouraging your child to attend the academic or student center and attend classes specifically designed to teach these skills. In addition, there are several books on the market that also teach learning skills for students.

Substance Abuse Issues

Substance misuse is a big topic and probably needs a book of its own to do this subject justice. However, what is most important to know is that drugs and alcohol can cause depression, anxiety, and other mental health issues in some individuals. That is why it is important to rule out the possibility of drugs and alcohol causing or worsening depression as soon as possible. Unfortunately, kids in college have greater access to alcohol and drugs, such as marijuana, ecstasy, and cocaine, and prescription drugs including benzodiazepines (Xanax, Valium and Klonopin), and simulants (Adderall and Ritalin). Drugs and alcohol – yes, marijuana too – can literally hijack the brain into thinking they are "helping" your child feel better; but in actuality, they may be making things worse. Your child might be hesitant to give up the drug or alcohol due to misperceptions about the substance's usefulness. However, it is almost impossible to diagnose someone's depression, anxiety, or anything else when that person is using alcohol or drugs regularly.

Signs and symptoms that point to possible substance abuse typically include sudden changes in mood (depression, anger, or irritability) or behaviors (increased oppositionality, isolation, and loss of friends or change in friend group). I tell parents, "If you say to yourself, 'This is totally out of character for our son or daughter,' you may want to consider that your child is using drugs and alcohol."

If I determine someone has a substance abuse problem, I almost always recommend abstinence or tapering off of the drugs and/or alcohol for a few months to get a sense of what someone's baseline is. I evaluate them over the next several months, making notes of the positive and negative (withdrawal symptoms) effects of abstinence. If the substance abuse issues are particularly severe, I will recommend a substance abuse treatment program, such as a detox or rehabilitation program, first.

One of the more difficult issues I will often run into when I am evaluating a college aged student is that they do not want their parents to know about their drug and/or alcohol abuse. As they are eighteen years of age or older, they are able to restrict the information I can provide to parents. In this case, I will spend a lot of time putting together a treatment plan for sobriety, build trust with the student, and then begin helping them talk with their parents about their use.

Another issue I run into is when a college-aged student denies substance misuse but is, in fact, regularly using. This can result in misdiagnosis and inappropriate treatments. Nondisclosure of substance misuse can also delay treatment, increase risk for side effects from medications that were not needed, and even cause death from the drugs of abuse or interactions with prescribed medications. I will let the student know about these risks when I assess for drug and alcohol misuse. I will always discuss this information with them alone and ensure confidentiality to promote trust, openness, and honesty.

The other issue I commonly run into is that your child may refuse to "give up" their drug of choice because "it's the only thing that helps me." I often let parents and students know that none of the treatments I might recommend (other than substance abuse treatment) will work if they are using. I tell them, "If you are using drugs or alcohol, then any treatment I give you is like peeing in the ocean." In other words, it's a waste of time and will not make a difference in life. With young adults, I try to provide education around the effects of drugs and alcohol on the brain and the resulting mood and anxiety symptoms. I will assess the pros and cons of using to get a better understanding of what the student likes and doesn't like about the drug/alcohol and discuss negative consequences of use. If the substance abuse is moderate to severe, I may start off by recommending a rehab program to address this issue first and foremost before discussing other treatment and schooling options.

Depression can be a symptom or it can be an illness. There are multiple causes of depression, and it is important to evaluate for any underlying biological reason for the depression, including medical causes. In addition, psychological factors such as temperament and personality traits, and social stress can also contribute to the feeling of depression or can exacerbate any underlying depressive disorder. At this age, transitioning to adulthood, meeting parental and personal expectations and peer issues are also key issues to evaluate as potential contributors to depression. Finally, learning disorders and substance abuse issues can also lead to symptoms of depression.

5

STEP 2:

Exploring Integrative Approaches to Treatment

In this chapter, I will be exploring integrative approaches to treat depression. I will be using a patient case example, Megan, to walk us through the evaluation and treatment process.

Megan

Megan is a nineteen-year-old female who came to my office with severe depression, including symptoms of low moods, severe anxiety and ruminations, poor to no appetite, low energy, suicidal thoughts, and an inability to get out of bed most days of the week. She returned home from school during her freshman year after her roommate notified the school about concerns that Megan was suicidal and depressed. The university notified Megan's parents, and she was sent home for treatment.

Megan had a long history of depression and was on multiple medications that always seem to work initially, but then stop working after two to three months. Megan was in and out of therapy since the age of thirteen to address issues related to anxiety, depression, and her mother's breast cancer diagnosis and treatment. Megan's depression was considered recurrent, severe, and treatment refractory (meaning she did not respond to medications and therapy in the past). A discussion regarding safety was the first step in Megan's evaluation.

Safety

One of the first things I evaluate when seeing someone with depression is severity. How urgent is the issue? Does he or she need a more intensive program, like an inpatient hospitalization, a residential treatment, a day treatment program, or a rehabilitation center? Most young adults can be treated in an outpatient setting. The top reasons for hospitalization or other more advanced forms of treatment include severe depression and inability to get out of bed, eat, or care for one's self; and suicidal thoughts and plans to carry out those thoughts. If a student cannot be trusted with his own safety, a safety plan cannot be reasonably put together, and parents or other caregivers are unable to monitor the young adult for twenty-four hours a day to maintain the child's safety, then hospitalization is often required. Other reasons include thoughts of wanting to harm others and psychotic symptoms, such as hearing or seeing things that are not there, paranoia, bizarre thoughts that could not possibly be true, and confused thinking. Manic symptoms can also necessitate hospitalization and may include feelings of euphoria and elevated moods; overconfidence; little to no sleep; high energy; talking fast and having ideas that seem to jump from topic to topic; high-risk behaviors, such as spending a lot of money; driving fast; and hypersexuality.

Both psychotic and manic symptoms can be seen in individuals that abuse drugs and alcohol. Again, I want to stress the need to rule out substance abuse issues to prevent erroneous diagnoses and treatments. If you have concerns as a parent that any of the above are going on, then taking your child to a crisis evaluation center or an ER for a safety evaluation is the first step in getting your child the treatment he needs.

The safety evaluation should always be performed by mental health professionals who are trained in identifying suicide risks and know how to put a safety plan in place. According to the Center for Disease Control, risk factors that put an individual at increased risk for suicide include prior suicide attempts; easy access to guns, pills, or other lethal means; a family member or friend dying by suicide; social isolation; bullying and poor family relationships; substance abuse issues; and chronic medical illness. Certain populations of individuals are also at risk, including gay, lesbian, bisexual, and transgender youth. Major losses, such as a breakup or loss of a loved one, legal issues, or exposure to violence and sexual assault/trauma are other major precipitating factors that can increase suicide risk. Protective factors that reduce suicide risk include having high-quality mental health treatment, having close relationships with family and friends, having good self-esteem and solid coping strategies, feeling optimistic and talking about the future and having cultural or religious beliefs that discourage suicide.

For Megan's evaluation, the safety discussion included an evaluation of the severity of her suicidal thoughts. During our initial interview, Megan discussed her thoughts of wanting to end her life, but she had no clear plan on how she would do this. Megan had no access to any weapons. Megan also reported she had no intent to act on her suicidal thoughts and had hope for the future and talked a lot about her plans over the next few years. She also felt a close-enough relationship with her parents to be open about her symptoms. She had a good network of friends at home and at school. Because Megan did not appear to be at high risk of suicide, we next put together a plan on what to do if her suicidal thoughts got worse, and who she would contact if this happened. Megan's parents were present during parts of the initial interview of the safety plan and both felt confident that they could ensure Megan was under close supervision. Based on her safety evaluation and plan, Megan was subsequently treated in an outpatient setting.

Severity of Symptoms

Once you know your child is safe, you can then begin assessing the severity of symptoms and current needs of your child. I am always thinking about both the short-term and long-term treatment options as I put together a treatment plan, but I always start with where the young adult is at "in this moment." I like to start at the severity of the depressive symptoms as this will help guide my recommendations now and in the future. I then will consider medical issues that could be contributing to his or her mental health issues. Next, I will focus on the impact of psychological factors and social issues on the child's current mental state. Finally, I will review the basic three pillars of brain health – diet, exercise, and sleep – for ways to improve on these key areas.

So, how do we assess severity outside of asking, "How bad is it?" First, we look at level of functioning – is your child able to go to school or work, do homework, get out of bed, brush his teeth, make himself food, or watch TV? I will also ask if your child is isolating himself from friends or family and if there is anything in life that he still enjoys doing. Is he eating or sleeping; and if so, is it too much or too little? All of these factors help to assess the severity of the depression. Once we know the severity, we can then start down the path of treatment options.

I typically would not consider treating severe depression with therapy, supplements, or diet alone. Severe depression comes with an increased risk for suicidality, dropping out of school, lost relationships, psychosis, and substance abuse. Also, I am a firm believer that it is just "bad for your brain" to be in a depressed state, so I tend to be more aggressive with my treatment plan when treating severe depression. I will often start with reviewing and choosing a medication plan that suits the child's needs. These most often include the antidepressant classes, but other types of medications can also be considered based on underlying issues. I will also discuss the non-medication-based treatment called Transcranial Magnetic Stimulation (TMS) treatment as well. At times, I will recommend both options, particularly if there is significant suicidal ideation and time is of the utmost importance. For individuals that struggle with milder to moderate depressive symptoms, treatment strategies involving nutrition, exercise, individual therapy, supplements, and sleep hygiene take a central role in my integrative treatment plan.

Biological Treatment Options

Megan's depression was determined to be severe and included symptoms of low moods, severe anxiety and ruminations, poor to no appetite, low energy, suicidal thoughts, and an inability to get out of bed most days of the week. She was in treatment for many years and was on many different types of medications, which were all ineffective. Based on her depression history, Megan and her parents chose to initially focus on biological treatments to rapidly improve her depression and suicidality. We first did a review of her medication history to get a better sense of what had worked in the past and what medications did not.

There are many different types and classes of medications that can be chosen to address the needs of an individual. If your child has tried several types of antidepressants and has either not responded or has struggled with side effects, pharmacogenomics testing can help pinpoint better medication options. This type of analysis looks at an individual's genes and provides feedback about which medications he or she may more likely respond to and tolerate with fewer side effects. Although this testing is not 100 percent accurate, it can help guide and eliminate potentially adverse effects from medications. This type of testing is readily available now, and some people choose to have this testing done before any medications are even tried. This is an individual choice and one to consider with your psychiatrist.

Many people are familiar with the application of antidepressants, such as fluoxetine, sertraline, etc., in the treatment of depression, but fewer are aware of the powerful non-medication-based treatment called transcranial magnetic stimulation (TMS). TMS is not electroconvulsive therapy (ECT) and should not be confused with this type of treatment. ECT is a procedure that is done under general anesthesia in a hospital setting and uses electricity to induce a seizure in the brain to "reset" it. ECT is a treatment reserved only for the most depressed individuals and can have significant side effects, such as memory issues. In contrast, TMS uses magnetic pulses to influence the firing pattern of specific brain networks that are involved in depression, anxiety, and executive functioning. This treatment is as effective – if not more effective – as antidepressants with relatively few to no side effects. The downsides of this treatment are cost, although insurance is covering this treatment more and more; and that it requires daily treatment (typically five days a week) over a six-week period of time. This is an outpatient procedure and no medications or sedations are used, so participants are able to drive themselves to and from their appointments daily. This treatment has other off-label applications as well and is used in the treatment of ADHD, anxiety, PTSD, and substance dependence, all of which are often co-occurring in individuals with depression.

In addition to the biological treatments as noted above, it is important to obtain and review laboratory findings and treat any nutritional or hormonal deficiencies such as low thyroid hormone, vitamin D, folate, or B12. If nutritional and hormonal deficits are not adequately treated, depression may not fully resolve. For the thyroid hormone in particular, inadequate evaluation and treatment can lead to improper treatment of depression and worsening moods.

Certain herbal products and supplement products can also be considered here as well. They can be powerful in reducing depression and anxiety symptoms, but they can also cause side effects by themselves or when interacting with other medications or supplements, so make sure you are taking them under the care of a physician.

I also recommend making sure your child is taking good quality products by checking out the website ConsumerLab.com. This site is like Consumer Reports (consumerreports.org) but for supplements, vitamins, and herbal products, and it independently tests products for quality and price. The site will also do side-by-side comparisons of supplements to help you make an informed decision when deciding between supplement brands.

Important herbal products and supplements utilized to address depression include St. John's wort (*Hypericum perforatum*), Rhodiola (*Rhodiola rosea*), S-adenosyl-methionine (SAMe), Omega-3 fatty acids, and 5-Hydroxytryptophan (5-HTP). St. John's wort is the most widely studied and used herbal product for the treatment of depressed mood. The mechanism of action is thought to be related to the herb causing changes in key neurotransmitters involved in depression. Because of the direct and indirect action on neurotransmitter systems in the brain, caution should be utilized if combining with other antidepressant medications and should only be done under doctor's supervision. Rhodiola is another botanical product that is reported to treat depression and decrease fatigue. There are only a few small studies assessing the impact of this herb on depression, and results are inconsistent.

Omega-3 fatty acids are long-chain fatty acids that are important for cell membrane function throughout the body including brain neurons. Incorporation of these healthy fatty acids in brain cell membranes is important for optimal brain functioning, and low levels of these fatty acids are associated with depression. Omega-3 fatty acids can be obtained through the diet via certain fish, such as salmon and sardines; and nuts/seeds, such as walnuts, flax, hemp, and chia seeds. Individuals with a poor diet are at risk of essential fatty acid deficiency – supplementing with fish oil pills, particularly in those struggling with depression, is easy and well-tolerated. I often use this complementary supplement for both its possible antidepressant effects and anti-inflammatory benefits as well.

Another supplement, S-adenosyl-methionine (SAMe), is an important amino acid obtained from high-protein foods, such as meat and fish; and as an over the counter supplement. This amino acid is important for brain functioning due to its involvement in cell membrane functioning and neurotransmitter (serotonin, dopamine, and norepinephrine) synthesis. SAMe is thought to aid in the treatment of depression due to a methylation process in concert with B-12 and folate, so optimal levels of these vitamins is important as well. 5-Hydroxytryptophan (5-HTP) is another supplement available on the market and is also an essential amino acid that is converted to serotonin in the body. Serotonin is thought to be a key player in moods, and supplementation with 5-HTP is thought to increase levels of this important neurotransmitter.

Inositol, part of the vitamin B-complex; and L-theanine, an amino acid that is found in the tea plant *Camellia sinensis*, are both utilized in the treatment of depression and anxiety. There are far fewer studies of these agents, but I found in some individuals that these agents can be helpful when added to other mainstream treatments. Other herbal supplements I commonly recommend for either anxiety or insomnia include chamomile (*Matricaria recutita*), lemon balm (*Melissa officinalis*), valerian (*Valeriana officinalis*) *and* kava (*Piper Methysticum*).

Returning to Megan's story, we did discuss biological options for her treatment to get her symptoms quickly under control.

She did not have a prior treatment with TMS, so I recommended two different types of treatment strategies, including a high-dose TMS treatment three times daily for three consecutive days to reduce/eliminate suicidal thoughts; followed by a once-daily treatment for six weeks to reduce/eliminate depression. During the six-week TMS treatment, she was weaned off medications that were ineffective.

After two weeks of TMS treatment, Megan's depression began to improve, and she was able to engage in other treatments. I evaluated for any medical or underlying issues, and a full set of laboratory assessments were obtained. Megan was found to be deficient in B12 and was a poor metabolizer of folate (MTFHR). She started on B12 supplementation and l-methylfolate. In addition, she was also started on two grams of omega-3 fatty acids. Finally, a probiotic was initiated to help with her digestive issues and gut health.

Other types of biological treatments that are at the top of my list for the treatment of depression are nutrition, exercise, and sleep hygiene. I will discuss these treatments in more detail below, but I will almost always include these types of treatment recommendations in my integrative treatment plan. I consider them "medicine" and prescribe them the same way I do medications. I do this because these treatments can be very effective for treating depression in certain individuals, preventing reoccurrence of depression in the future, and improving resiliency from life stress. When prescribing these interventions, I take into consideration what the individual is ready for. For example, telling someone who is so depressed they cannot get out of bed to start exercising daily is not going to be achievable, and I don't like to set people up for failure. Similarly, I would not ask someone without an appetite to start immediately incorporating more plant-based meals at least five times a week. The important piece is to figure out what each individual *can* and is *willing* to do *now* to get them on the road to recovery. Then, as your child recovers, I would adjust the diet and exercise regimen to their level of comfort.

Meditation is another form of treatment that I will often recommend to patients, particularly if there is a high anxiety component. Meditation is shown to affect key brain networks that are involved in depression and anxiety. Done consistently over time, meditation can change the architecture of brain networks in a positive and sustained way. There are many types of meditation out there and trying out different types to find a "good fit" is important. The key to mediation is to demystify and simplify it so that it is knowable, doable, practical, and not too "woo woo" for each particular individual.

I often teach a simple yet powerful meditation I learned from the Deepak Chopra Center that utilizes a personalized mantra-based mediation based on the vibrational sound of the universe during the time of a person's birth. This type of meditation focuses on a repetitive sound/mantra to clear one's thoughts, improve focus, and help one reach deeper levels of awareness. I will start by having individuals do this simple meditation practice for five minutes a day, when they are ready, and remind them to be gentle with themselves and be confident that they are doing it exactly right. I will increase the meditation time to thirty to sixty minutes as an individual grows confidence in their meditation practice.

Another type of popular meditation includes mindfulness meditation, which focuses on an object or the breath and instructs you to allow thoughts to move easily through your head without judgement or paying any particular attention to them. Sound-based and movement-based meditations, such as yoga and *qigong*, are other great mediation options that can be useful for individuals who struggle with quieting the mind or who gain greater peace with movement.

For Megan, we first began with a mantra-based meditation and then moved to a mindfulness-based meditation. Megan struggled to quiet her mind with both of these types of meditations because she had significant anxiety and ruminating thoughts that were distracting. So, we switched to movement-based meditation – yoga – to get her more focused on movement to aide in calming her mind. After several months, Megan retried mindfulness meditation, focusing instead on breathing, and had a greater success with this technique overall.

An additional complementary approach to depression in the biological category includes light therapy. Light therapy is early-morning, artificial exposure to bright light for an average of thirty to sixty minutes daily. The therapy utilizes a light box. Light therapy is shown to improve depression and is especially beneficial in improving seasonal depression, which occurs in the fall and winter. The Center for Environmental Therapeutics recommends the following criteria for light box selection:

- The box should provide 10,000 lux of illumination at a comfortable sitting distance.
- Fluorescent lamps should have a smooth diffusing screen that filters out ultraviolet (UV) rays. UV rays are harmful to the eyes and skin.
- The lamps should give off white light rather than colored

light. "Full spectrum" lamps and blue (or bluish) lamps provide no known therapeutic advantage.

- The light should be projected downward toward the eyes at an angle to minimize aversive visual glare.
- Smaller is not better. When using a compact light box, even small head movements will take the eyes out of the therapeutic range of the light

Non-Biological Treatment Options

The non-biological treatments for depression typically include therapies, such as individual, family, and group therapies. Within each class of therapies, there are many subtypes of therapies with many different and confusing acronyms, such as supportive therapy, cognitive behavioral therapy (CBT), dialectic behavioral therapy (DBT), and Eye Movement Desensitization Reprocessing (EMDR), etc. Because of the vast types of therapies available, it is important to work with a professional who is knowledgeable in what each of these therapies are, who they are most useful for, and which therapists in the area are adept at delivering them. If you are starting from square one and do not know who or what to start with, calling around and interviewing several therapists and discussing your child's needs would be a good first step. You can ask what the therapist's qualifications are, their training type, and what approach the therapist would use in treating your child. In general, most therapists are trained in a variety of techniques and use a blended approach to therapy. In other words, most therapists will use a combination of strategies based on a client's needs and will change the strategies as needed. As an example, a therapist might start seeing a client and begin with supportive therapy to start the process of understanding the presenting issues and help to establish trust in the relationship. Over time, the therapist may begin DBT if the client needs help developing coping skills to help manage moods or maladaptive behaviors; or, alternatively, the therapist may start CBT when her client is ready to challenge problematic thoughts and beliefs.

Next, it would be important to have your child meet with one to three therapists for an interview and find one who he or she connects with. Trust and a connection are the most important elements in therapy, so ask your child who he or she likes and resonates with the most before moving forward.

Finally, it is important to develop a schedule and appropriate frequency of therapy visits to make sure your child can be seen regularly and for a desired duration of time. For therapy to be successful, building a strong therapeutic relationship with a therapist is one of the most important pieces. Having a regular, frequent, and consistent therapy schedule is one way to ensure this relationship is established quickly and that the therapeutic work that needs to be done progresses in a timely manner.

Family therapy is typically recommended if there is turmoil within the family structure that is holding your child back from succeeding as a young adult in college. Typical issues could include marital strife or a divorce between parents, medical or mental illness in a parent or sibling, and communication breakdowns between child and parents. Family discord can bring up feelings of anger, grief, anxiety, and ultimately guilt for your child if they are worried about leaving the family during a time of crisis. These feelings, combined with the stress of transitioning to college and adulthood, can trigger depressive symptoms.

Group therapy for college-aged students is another great resource for those students, particularly if they occur in the academic setting. It reinforces the idea that the student is not alone, and it increases social connectedness.

From a psychological perspective, one key element that impacted Megan's recovery from depression was family dynamic issues related to her mother's cancer diagnosis and treatments. Her individual work focused on her fear of losing her mom and her fear the cancer would come back. She also worked through anger at being her mom's primary caretaker, guilt about being angry at her parents for having to fill the caretaker role, and sadness over missing out on fun high-school experiences. Megan felt she knew who she was and had a strong sense of identity, but felt it was hard to leave home and go off to school and not keep fulfilling the role of caretaker.

In family sessions, I met with her parents alone to discuss the impact of Mom's cancer diagnosis for the couple. The couple strengthened the emotional connection between themselves and helped identify mixed messages they may be sending to their daughter that prevented her from moving forward independently as an adult. In family sessions, we addressed the impact of Mom's cancer diagnosis on the family, the roles of family members in the family system, and how to change these roles.

Treatment Options for Substance Abuse

Alcohol and drugs greatly impact moods and make treatment of depression near impossible. Again, assessing the severity of substance misuse is key in determining what the next best steps are for treatment. Treatment options range from inpatient detox, thirty-day rehabilitation programs, intensive outpatient programs, substance abuse counseling, and Alcoholic Anonymous/Narcotics Anonymous options. In each program, it is important to treat both the substance abuse and mental health issues, with the priority focusing on achieving sobriety and assessing mental health issues during this process. The key here is abstinence from all substances of abuse for at least three to six months so effective evaluation and treatment of depression can be undertaken.

Back to the Basics – Diet, Exercise, and Sleep

Diet

Diet and nutrition are integral components in any treatment plan. Depression is commonly associated with overeating or undereating due to appetite changes. It is common for individuals with depression to have carbohydrate cravings and cravings for high fat "comfort foods," such as ice cream, chips, macaroni and cheese, pizza, and candy. These types of foods impact the brain by causing a release of dopamine from your reward centers that can give you a feeling of temporary relief from depression but are nutritionally void. Alternatively, depression can lead to poor appetite due to feelings of nausea, abdominal discomfort, and fullness, thereby leading to poor nutrition overall. Without proper nutrition, the body and brain do not produce the vital hormones, neurotransmitters, and biochemical energy that is needed for recovery from depression. For example, if you don't get enough of certain amino acids and B-vitamins, you may not produce or metabolize key neurotransmitters, such as serotonin and dopamine in the brain. These neurotransmitters are implicated in depression and are often the targets for medication-based therapies. In addition, poor neuronal cell membrane function due to poor fatty acid composition or inadequate protein complexes can also lead to dysfunctional neural cell signaling and can also impact overall mental health and cognition. Because of the importance of proper nutrition on overall brain health, I will often recommend a good multivitamin with minerals and supplements, such as omega-3 fatty acids to ensure appropriate daily essentials are met. Then, I will work on incorporating more healthy foods and meals into the diet depending on needs and dietary preferences.

Another reason to evaluate diet is to identify if there are any dietary habits that are leading to increased inflammation in the body. Processed foods; meats; sugar; and specific food allergies or intolerances – wheat, dairy, eggs, or nuts – could be leading to inflammation in the body. Inflammation is thought to contribute to depression, and identification and elimination of any causes is key in helping your child heal from depression.

Inflammation can have many causes, including trauma, stress, inflammatory disorders, or gut-biome disruption. It is thought to increase inflammatory chemicals in the blood that can disrupt the blood-brain barrier, leading to brain inflammation and ultimately depressive symptoms. In fact, in a pivotal study by Setiawan and associates published in *JAMA* in 2015, individuals with depression were found to have up to 33 percent more inflammation than nondepressed individuals.

Diet can not only cause inflammation but can also reduce inflammation. Healthy eating of foods rich in antioxidants;

polyphenols; and good fats, such as those high in omega-3 fatty acids, can significantly reduce inflammation throughout the body. The types of foods that contain these vital anti-inflammatory benefits include fruit and vegetables, nuts and seeds, and dark chocolate. To maximize the benefits of fruits and vegetables, one should eat a large variety of these foods and across the rainbow of colors. Herbal teas are another good source of antioxidants as well.

If your child suffers from other underlying inflammatory illnesses at baseline, such as inflammatory bowel syndrome, Crohn's disease, rheumatological illnesses, etc. he or she should be particularly cautious about diet. I typically start by recommending removing common offenders of inflammation, including sugary foods and drinks and processed foods. Next, if inflammation is still suspected, I will prescribe an elimination diet or, alternatively, will remove certain foods one at a time to see if an underlying cause can be determined. In addition, for some individuals with depression, I will often recommend diets rich in antioxidants, as noted above; and supplements found to reduce inflammation, such as curcumin and omega-3 fatty acids.

Regarding Megan's diet, she described herself as eating a vegan diet that included a significant amount of processed and high carbohydrate foods. However, due to her worsening depression over the past few months, she was struggling to eat and had no appetite. She reported her diet consisted of high-sugar beverages and foods, including soda and candy. She also did not feel she was eating more than 1000 calories a day and felt "full" and "sick to her stomach" often. Megan had a Body Mass Index (BMI) of seventeen, which meant she was significantly underweight.

For the initial treatment plan, I recommended a minimum of 1500 calories a day – that included multiple light meals and snacks. To help with feelings of fullness, I asked her to sip smoothies made with spinach, kale, berries, and almond milk with additives like nut butters, hemp seeds, chia seeds, and ground flax seed for extra nutrients. I recommended vegetable soups, broth, hummus, vegan yogurt and berries, fruits, handfuls of nuts and seeds, nut butters on toast, etc. Higher carb meals and not eating after 7 p.m. were recommended for her last meal to help with sleep. In addition, over time, as Megan's depression improved and as her appetite improved, we focused more on whole plant-based meals with fewer processed foods, reduced sodas, and less high-sugar foods.

Exercise

Exercise is an important component of any treatment plan for depression. Exercise causes a natural release of endorphins, our natural happy hormones secreted by the brain that improve our mood and reduce pain. In addition, exercise also reduces the stress hormones adrenaline and cortisol, which also helps to reduce anxiety and depressive symptoms.

Exercise was also found to release brain-derived neurotropic factor (BDNF). BDNF is important for healthy brain neurons and synaptic plasticity, which is important for optimal brain function. Reduced brain levels of BDNF are associated with Alzheimer's, depression, and anxiety. In addition to exercise, certain diets, such as intermittent fasting; and serotonin reuptake inhibitor antidepressant medications, such as sertraline, have also been found to increase BDNF levels in the brain.

One of the issues that comes up with individuals with depression is that they often struggle with low energy and motivation, making it difficult to engage in exercise. So, again, it is important to meet your child where he is at and start a program based on what he can do now. For instance, in an individual with severe depression, I would start out by having him get up every day and open the blinds to all his windows. Then, we would progress to going outside in the midday sun and sitting for five to ten minutes. As he is beginning to feel better, I will ask him to walk for five minutes and build this up over time. For individuals with mild to moderate depression, I might ask them, "What do you think you could do right now?" If that is fifteen minutes three times a week, then we start there. I will ask about interests, such as hiking, biking, basketball, mountain climbing, or skiing, as it's easier to exercise when you are doing something you enjoy. Finally, I always recommend outside exercise when it's sunny and encourage exercise in beautiful environments to get some "nature therapy."

For Megan's exercise plan, we examined her prior exercise habits and found out she used to be a competitive cross-country track runner in high school but stopped running when she went to college. She indicated a desire to start running again and admitted a lack of exercise was "making things worse." After two weeks of treatment, we slowly began integrating a program to get her out of the house and walking outside for five to ten minutes a day. Her exercise program was then increased, as tolerated, for the remainder of her treatment. By six months, she was back to running three to five miles five times a week. Her exercise was performed no later than 3 p.m. to avoid causing sleep issues later in the evening. In addition to running, Megan also started performing yoga three times a week as described earlier – she found it was more of a meditative practice.

Sleep

Sleep is a very important factor when treating depression and is also commonly impacted in depression. Your daughter or son may sleep too much or too little. Improving sleep by normalizing duration and quality can have dramatic benefits on mood. In fact, I often find that if I can get someone to sleep normally, I can more easily treat his or her depression. Reviewing sleep schedule, naps, temperature of the bedroom, use of electronics or TV in the bedroom, and timing of last meals are important factors to consider.

There are some very effective herbal products – Valerian root, Lemon balm, Lavender, Chamomile and Hops – that can aid in individuals who struggle with mild to moderate sleep difficulties. Supplements, like melatonin, L-theanine, and magnesium, can also be effective.

Furthermore, progressive muscle relaxation techniques and guided sleep meditations can also be effective. Progressive muscle relaxation is a technique where one tightens one major muscle group in the body moving from the head to the toes. One is asked to progressively tighten these major muscles groups one at a time for about five seconds and then relax the muscles for another five to ten seconds before moving on to another major muscle group. Once completed, an individual typically is both physically and mentally relaxed and ready for sleep. Simply search "progressive muscle relaxation" online for free videos and scripts that can be easily downloaded and incorporated in your sleep regimen. Sleep-guided meditations are also available online, as are instructor guided meditations that help you relax and fall asleep by quieting the mind.

Finally, for moderate to severe sleep difficulties, I do often recommend the temporary use of non-addictive medications for sleep. Low doses of non-addictive medications, such as gabapentin and trazodone, are non-habit forming, can be taken only as needed, and can easily be stopped without major withdrawal issues. I find that as the depression improves, most individuals will be able to reduce and ultimately eliminate the need for sleep medication.

For Megan's treatment, I was able to address her sleep issues by reviewing her sleep history, including night rituals, electronic usage, temperature of room, and sleep patterns. Megan was staying in her bed most of the day and taking several naps. She was on her phone and viewing social media and YouTube videos most of the day as well. Her room temperature was set at 72 degrees. Megan was unable to fall asleep for two hours most nights and woke up frequently throughout the night.

Megan's sleep recommendations included getting out of bed and moving to the living room during the day. She was placed on a sleep schedule and asked to not nap at all during the day, which was only possible after her second week of treatment. Her bedroom temperature was set to 68 degrees, and she was asked to limit social media to one or two hours a day. She was taught progressive muscle relaxation exercises to help her relax at bedtime and was asked to take three to five milligrams of melatonin thirty to sixty minutes before bedtime to help with falling and staying asleep.

There are a wide variety of mainstream and complementary treatment options for depression that can be individualized to help your child overcome depression. Choosing treatments based on severity of symptoms and meeting you child where he or she is at right now will help you put together an integrative treatment plan that is effective and achievable. It is important to not overwhelm individuals struggling with depression. Not all of the treatments listed need to be undertaken, and I typically construct a treatment plan that starts small and expands upon itself as your child improves. I find small changes in a few key areas, such as sleep, diet, and exercise, will synergistically impact other areas and lead to an exponential improvement in moods.

6

STEP 3:

Educational Autopsy

College can be an amazing experience for your child and is full of academic and personal growth. Graduating college can set your child up for a successful career that will enable them to provide for themselves financially in the future. However, college can also be stressful. There are new surroundings, new routines, new freedoms, and new friends to be made. Academically, there are greater expectations, harder classes, and the need for individual motivation to get homework and assignments done. Each of these changes can lead to feelings of being overwhelmed, stressed, isolated, and unsure of how to move forward or get the help needed. Therefore, I generally like to get a sense of "what went wrong" and "what went right" while in college. I start by evaluating the current college or university your child selected, and I like to ask the following questions:

- Why did you choose this college or university? Culture? Academics? Environment?
- What were your expectations and hopes about this school?
- Do you like the size of your school, or is it too big or too small?

- Are the class sizes too big or small for you?
- How are the professors?
- Are the academic requirements what you anticipated? Too hard? Too easy?
- Do you like the location?
- Are you doing well in your classes?
- What do you like most about your school?
- What do you like least about your school?
- Do you want to go back to that same school?

After I get a sense of what your child did or did not like about college, I then try to get a better assessment about friends and social supports. I want to really get a sense of your child's connections at school and tease out feelings of loneliness, isolation, and not "fitting in." Here are some examples of questions I ask:

- Do you feel like you fit in there?
- Do you like the culture of the school now?
- Are you able to make friends?
- Do you live in a dorm, and do you like your roommates?
- Do you belong or participant in any sports, clubs, or social groups?
- Who do you talk to on a regular basis at school?
- Do you feel alone sometimes?

These questions can lead you and your child to determine if this college or university is the right fit for your child and whether or not a future change in schooling is necessary.

Next, I evaluate the current mental health support at your child's university or college. Not all academic institutions are created equal in this regard, and there are varying degrees of mental health support at any given school. Some institutions have built-in mental health clinics that staff full-time mental health professionals and are easily accessible. However, other institutions may only have limited mental health resources and can only provide therapy services for a certain number of sessions (e.g., five sessions a year). You may also encounter academic institutions that refer their students to outside local practitioners.

Knowing what is available at your child's current school and whether or not the resources are adequate will help aid the process of transition back to college. You will need to decide if the resources at school can meet your child's needs. If not, you will need to explore what other mental health professionals are available in the area that could support your child while in college. In other words, a lack of a cohesive mental health program at college could lead to recommendations about changing the college/university or to establishing care with outside providers prior to returning to college.

Assessing the academic support programs or accommodation programs is another step toward determining whether your child's current academic placement is a good fit. Academic support centers can provide a variety of support, including academic advising, tutoring, and peer mentorship. They can have classes focused on time management, test taking, study skills, and test prep. These services are available to all students and can be very supportive for students struggling academically. Accommodation centers provide additional services to those with disabilities and mental health issues. Colleges are required by law to provide support for students with disabilities and mental health issues; however, the extent and variety of services available can vary between schools. Contact the academic or accommodations department to see what services are available. It is important to determine what support your child can get for both learning issues, e.g., ADHD or dyslexia, and mental health issues, such as depression. Parents should specifically ask 1) what paperwork should be completed and 2) which outside letters of support (doctors or therapists) are also needed for their child to obtain additional accommodations. Typically, letters from a therapist or psychiatrist and/or prior neuropsychological testing are needed in order to obtain additional accommodation services.

Some examples of accommodations that can be made available include:

- Increased testing times (e.g., time and a half on exams)
- Taking exams in a separate room
- The ability to reschedule exams if the student has too many exams within a small period of time
- The ability to leave class sometimes for a few minutes for a "mental refresher"
- Note taking and a LiveScribe pen for taking notes in class
- Reduced course load with full-time equivalency
- Flexibility with deadlines and due dates
- Housing accommodations (e.g., private room)

Again, most of these accommodations will need supporting documentation from mental health professionals addressing why your child needs and would benefit from these accommodations.

Finally, during the "educational autopsy," I want to get a sense of whether an academic leave is required, and, if so, for how long. This is usually determined by the severity of the depression and predicted response to treatment. However, academic institutions have their own rules and regulations about how students can take a leave of absence from school, especially if mid-term. It is important to contact the school to get clear guidelines for academic withdrawal and understand your child's rights and responsibilities both financially and academically, in order to safely withdrawal without penalty. If your child has already withdrawn from school, it is still important to know what can be done now to protect your child academically due to the withdrawal and once he or she returns to school. Most institutions will work with you to ensure your child does not suffer academically due to his or her depression, but letting the institutions know sooner rather than later can make sure everything that can be done will be done.

Having a mental health care provider help with letters of need/support can be instrumental in getting your child the academic leave that is necessary. The mental health professional will need to document the medical necessity of your child's leave of absence from school and to provide a written letter to the school.

It is also important to discuss what the expectations are of the school before they will accept your child back into college. Some schools may require a return to school form by a mental health professional that states your child is ready and able to come back safely to the college or university. The schools may also require your child be seen in the student mental health center or have established care with mental health providers in the community.

Finally, you will want to make sure you are aware of how long a leave of absence from the college your child can have before they are automatically withdrawn. This information can typically be obtained from the Office of Registrar or the Office of the Dean of Students.

Armed with the knowledge of "what worked" and "what did not" at your child's school, combined with the mental health and academic resources available to your child, you will have the important information for whether your child should set a goal to return to their current college or seek out a more suitable college once their depression is resolved. This information will allow you to seek out a more suitable college that meets more of the requirements and needs of your child.

7

STEP 4:

Assessing Developmental Factors Unique to Your Young Adult

Young adulthood typically describes individuals between the ages of eighteen and twenty-one years of age. At this stage of development, cognitive, emotional, social, and sexual development are continuing to occur. Each person matures in these domains at a different rate, often nonlinear, and at different ages. Cognitively, most young adults' brains will not reach full maturity until their mid-20s. Important cognitive functions that are still developing at this time include executive functioning skills like the ability to plan for the future, problem-solving, and decision-making. Specifically, young adults are making plans about their future and making informed decisions about what their long-term goals in life are going to be. Cognitive immaturity and developmental disorders, such as ADHD, can cause a delay in these cognitive abilities. Furthermore, depression can worsen cognition, making even simple decisions difficult and overwhelming. Abstract ideas, future planning, and difficult course work will task even the most cognitively intact young adult at this age.

Psychosocial Development

Psychological and emotional development are key areas of development occurring in young adults. According to the theorist Erik Erikson, there are eight psychosocial stages throughout the lifespan, and failure to master each developmental stage can cause difficulties in the next stage. Young adults are on the tail end of the identity vs. role confusion phase (ages twelve to eighteen) and the beginning of intimacy vs. isolation (20s through early 40s). In identity vs. role confusion, adolescents are attempting to develop a sense of self. This includes figuring out who they are and what they want their adult life to look like. Difficulties at this stage can lead to not knowing who they are or what they want in life, causing confusion about the future. Parents who are overly involved; have high expectations that exceed their child's wishes; or apply pressure to conform to parental ideas about occupation, sexuality, relationships, religion, or other issues can contribute to a weak sense of self and feelings of inadequacy and not knowing how to move forward in life.

Without knowledge of who you are, it makes the transition to the next stage –intimacy vs. isolation – more difficult. This stage is when young adults begin developing close relationships with peers and romantic partners. However, if a young adult has not successfully completed the stages prior, he may have trouble developing and maintaining successful relationships with others, leading to feelings of loneliness and social alienation. Not fitting in, not developing a peer group, or not being able to develop solid connections with peers or love interests can also be risk factors for the development of depression.

Culture

Cultural differences between parents and youths, especially if your child is the first person in your family to grow up in the U.S., can be difficult to navigate. Growing up in a different country with a different value system than one's parents can cause confusion about which culture, if any, your child fits into. Cultural differences between parents and their children that can lead to conflict include importance of family vs. importance of individuality, gender role expectations, acceptance of mental health issues, work ethic, and types of treatment approaches (e.g., western vs. eastern medicine).

Lee, an eighteen-year-old Chinese student who was the first in his family to be raised in America, struggled significantly with the transition between American and Chinese culture. He was raised to focus on the family's greater good and less on what he wanted as an individual. He was to work hard, attend an ivy league college, go on to medical school, and be successful for his family. However, as Lee grew up in the U.S., he was surrounded by an opposing culture where individuality was regarded more highly than family. He began to feel he could and should make his own choices and started expressing his own desires to his family. His parents were notably upset and disappointed in their son, and significant conflict developed between them. Lee felt sadness for not being able to pursue his own life goals and shame for being "the black sheep" of the family. His conflicting struggles between self-fulfillment and family obligations led him into a deep depression.

Sexuality

Sexuality can also be a source of stress depending on the community one grows up in and the level of acceptance in one's family. Gay, lesbian, bisexual, transgender, questioning/queer (LGBTQ+) individuals often struggle with high levels of anxiety and depression from an early age. According to the National Alliance on Mental Illness, LGBTQ+ individuals are more than twice as likely to have a mental health issue and are at a two to five times higher risk for suicide. There are many reasons for these concerning statistics, and they include parental, religious, and societal expectations that lead to a child feeling they have to hide their true identity, feel ashamed of who they are, and fear others will find out and reject them. They often also fear becoming a target of bullying and even violence. Even if a child's family is supportive, ongoing societal discrimination is still present and can impact a youth's emotional well-being and how they see themselves in the world.

Spirituality

Finally, spirituality is another area to explore. Individuals who lost their faith or spirituality often find that they have opposing views to their parents on spirituality or feel their faith in some way failed them, and they often find themselves with depression symptoms.

For Seth, his depression started shortly after he was told he would be excommunicated from his Church for being gay. Seth was a twenty-year-old gay male who was raised in a very religious family. He was also very religious and believed in the teachings of his church on everything "but being gay." He always felt very close to his God, church, and community, and he felt like he had a purpose in this community. He prayed for years to be heterosexual and "normal." When he came out to his parents, they took him to the church's pastor and were told he had to give up "being gay" or he could no longer be part of the church. As he knew he could not pretend to be heterosexual, he had to walk away from the church and community he had loved and thrived in his whole life. Despite his family's support, he felt rejected by his church and God and developed symptoms of depression related to grief and loss that lasted several years.

Coping Strategies

The development and utilization of coping strategies is also an important aspect when discussing depression. As we move from childhood to adolescence, we typically develop more mature and efficient ways to manage stress. However, problems in development, environment, or major stressful events can lead to maladaptive coping strategies that can cause significant problems in young adulthood. Examples of maladaptive coping strategies include over- or under-eating, avoidance of problems or blaming of problems on others, addiction issues, and self-harm behaviors. These maladaptive strategies may help in the moment, but long-term they can become major issues that can contribute to relationship difficulties, shame, body issues, and depression.

Assessing and replacing maladaptive strategies with healthy strategies to manage stress can make a significant impact on your child's emotional health. Some examples of healthy coping strategies include listening to music, reading, exercising, calling a trusted friend or family member, meditation, replacing negative thoughts with positive thoughts, and practicing gratitude.

In addition, it's also important to do an assessment of triggers for stress to see if certain issues keep coming up that can be addressed to help reduce stress overall.

Important family dynamics can contribute to difficulties in development or can cause difficulties leaving the nest. Divorce, domestic violence, having a medically ill parent or sibling, or having a family member with significant mental health or substance abuse issues that impacts other family members can cause your child to not want to progress in life. They might have fears of what will happen when they are away from the home or have guilt about leaving a parent or sibling(s) behind when the home life is chaotic.

As a parent, it is important to internally reflect on whether you gave your child permission, verbally and nonverbally, that it is okay to move on. Ask yourself how much you depend on them for emotional support, safety, medical care, care of siblings, and maintaining the home. Your child could be conflicted about leaving you or their siblings to manage without them and may not be able to focus on college. This could lead to feelings of both anger and resentment on the one hand and guilt and anxiety on the other. These feelings can also contribute to feelings of anxiety and depression.

In this chapter, you learned that there are many developmental and psychosocial factors that could be contributing to your child's depression and school failure. It is important to assess developmental stages and psychosocial factors that can be addressed to aid in your child moving forward as an adult and completing college. It should be noted that delays in development are not necessarily abnormal – different people develop differently over time and in different ways. Helping your child identify areas he may be "stuck" at and identifying the role you as the parent play in the transition to adulthood are key to launching your child successfully in college, adulthood, and beyond.

8

STEP 5:

So, What's the Plan? Treatment Plan for Depression

Integral to a holistic and collaborative treatment plan is understanding where your child is at right now and what the root cause of their depressive symptoms is, and then making an informed plan based on your child's future goals and wishes for themselves. Focusing on the basics of sleep, diet, and exercise will provide your child with an important foundation for future health and help improve long-term outcomes. Having a healthy brain and body will not only serve to improve treatment response now but will also lead to improved resiliency and protection from future mental health issues in the future. The timeline for treatment planning is typically dependent on the severity of the depression and future academic needs. I find that patience is critical at this point because you do not want to rush the process and set your child up for another failure. A loss of a school year at the beginning of your child's academic career should not be considered a setback and should be treated as a learning event. In order to show the key factors to consider in a treatment plan, I will illustrate one patient example that focuses on key issues that were important to address.

Joe

Joe is a nineteen-year-old Latin American male who recently left college for the second time in two years due to depression symptoms: moderate sadness, loss of interest, very low energy, overeating, and sleeping too much. Joe was failing classes and not doing schoolwork because he "just didn't care." He also did not have friends at school and described himself as shy, introverted, and afraid to talk to girls. He also admitted to struggles with anxiety and was not sure how to manage the anxiety outside of avoidance.

He called his parents and asked if he could leave school – he just could not cope academically and was "too stressed" all the time. He denied having suicidal thoughts, but just stated he "wanted to give up.... I will never achieve anything." Joe did not experience depression before college but struggled with it over the past one-and-a-half years since attending college.

His father was a very successful physician who emigrated from South America to escape corruption and poverty. He worked hard to make a successful life for him and his family. Both parents admit that they pushed Joe to be successful, and throughout high school, the only focus was on building his "college resume." Joe reports he was involved in a lot of clubs, sports, and academic teams, but didn't like *anything* he was doing in high school and was "too busy" to make or spend time with friends. "I was just doing what I was told by my parents. I didn't think for myself."

Six months ago, Joe started on one medication for depression, and he felt it helped "a little." Joe was significantly overweight. With a BMI of thirty-three, he had centralized obesity (high level of fat distribution around his midsection) and admitted to overeating high-fat and high-sugar foods. He was not exercising and stated that the only thing he enjoyed was video games and smoking marijuana. He admitted he was smoking almost daily to help with stress and anxiety before he returned home three weeks ago but did not have any marijuana since. Despite being clean from marijuana, his depression and anxiety, low motivation, and low energy persisted.

At initial assessment, Joe had no acute safety issues to address, so we discussed other biological treatments, such as medications like antidepressants; and supplements, such as SAM-e and St Johns Wart. Joe felt that his fatigue was so severe that unless he was treated, he would not be able to engage in any other treatment recommendations. We therefore started him on an antidepressant medication that helped with energy levels and motivation. He agreed to stop using marijuana for the next three to six months to help take an important variable out of the picture. On a laboratory evaluation, Joe had elevated cholesterol, high blood sugar, and elevated inflammatory markers. His laboratory work was consistent with metabolic syndrome and systemic inflammation, which put him at high risk for diabetes and cardiovascular disease in the future. He was placed on omega-3 fatty acids and curcumin to help with lipids and inflammation.

For Joe, he was sleeping ten to twelve hours a day and did not have trouble falling asleep or staying asleep. He had a hard time getting out of bed and never felt fully rested despite getting more than enough sleep. Because of his severe fatigue, obesity, and not feeling rested after ten or more hours of sleep, he was sent for a sleep study to be evaluated for obstructive sleep apnea. He was found to not have this sleep disorder.

Joe did have varying sleep patterns and typically went to bed anywhere between midnight and 2 a.m., then slept in until late morning to early afternoon. We started out his sleep hygiene by putting him on a set sleeping schedule – always going to bed at 11 p.m. and getting out of bed as soon as he woke up – so as not to drift off back to sleep. We discussed no video games, social media, or phone time after 9 p.m. As Joe started feeling better overall, we incorporated a consistent awake time and exercise regimen shortly after waking up.

We also discussed different dietary options and the impact his diet had on his moods, inflammation, and overall health. Joe described himself as a "meat eater" and not interested in eating vegetables or fruit. So, to begin his work, we started with reducing his carbohydrate intake to less than 100 grams per day, eliminating processed foods and high-sugar beverages, eating clean grass-fed meats and wild-caught salmon, and introducing intermittent fasting. An intermittent fasting program, based on the work by Jason Fung, was selected in combination with a low carbohydrate diet to help with weight loss, improve insulin resistance, and ultimately protect against the development of diabetes. For Joe, intermittent fast was slowly introduced by having him eating during fewer hours during the day. He started out by "fasting" for twelve hours – between 7 p.m. and 7 a.m. This was gradually increased (over a one-month period) to fasting for sixteen hours a day, between 7 p.m. and 11 a.m., and eating during an eight-hour period of time. Over time, as Joe started feeling better, had more energy, lost weight, and had more motivation, we introduced going without meat one to two days a week and had him experiment with trying different types of vegetables.

An exercise routine was incorporated into Joe's plan around week two. He was starting to feel a little better and was able to start getting outside and walking the dog every morning. He worked up to walking forty-five minutes a day with his dog. He then incorporated weightlifting exercises three times a week after five weeks of treatment.

Joe was also given two different skills to begin addressing his anxiety. One was a breathing technique that was to be performed twice a day and then again as needed for anxiety. In addition, Joe was introduced to meditation practice at week two. He incorporated five minutes of meditation twice daily and his meditation practice was increased to twenty to thirty minutes twice a day over the next several months.

From a developmental standpoint, Joe appeared to struggle with identity of self and not knowing what he wanted in life. He felt he could not stand up to his parents and was moving through life based on his parent's wishes. Joe felt that because his dad had such a tough life due to migrating to the United States and worked so hard to be successful, any complaint would be "ridiculous" because he had such an easy life in comparison. He also stated that his father's culture did not really understand or accept depression, particularly in men, so he felt "judged as weak" whenever he talked to his dad about his depression.

Since he did not develop a sense of who he was, what he enjoyed in life, and what he wanted to become as an adult, he felt very underprepared for the psychological and academic requirements of becoming an adult. He was also unable to establish either superficial or intimate peer relationships, therefore felt isolated, lonely, and depressed. To cope, he acquired unhealthy coping strategies, such as overeating and avoiding of anything that caused him anxiety, which contributed to feelings of poor self-esteem and low self-worth. Due to these struggles, Joe was seen for individual therapy twice weekly to begin learning about who he was and what he wanted out of life. He began exploring his wishes and desires, likes and dislikes, and exploring different possible extracurricular interests. Joe was taught to separate from his parents and begin trusting his own thoughts and feelings.

Joe practiced various social situations, first in the office and then in the real world. He was tasked to explore new experiences, from cooking classes to mountain biking. He took a few classes at a local community college to practice talking to other students, particularly girls. He also started working at a coffee shop to increase his social skills with a wide variety of people. Finally, Joe learned how to talk to his dad and teach him about depression, and ultimately felt respected and supported by him.

Joe's treatment occurred over the course of one year. His depression resolved fully within six months and was ultimately only on SAM-e and omega-3 fatty acids prior to returning to school 1 year later. He lost 50 lbs. that year and became an avid mountain biker and snowboarder. His laboratory studies returned to normal; he was no longer pre-diabetic; and he was at a healthy BMI of twenty-two. Joe considered going back to school after six months but instead wanted to work on improving his social skills and learning more about what he wanted for himself in the future, so he delayed his return to school for another 6 months.

9

STEP 6:

So, What's the Plan?
Back to School

In Chapter 6, we did an educational autopsy to determine what "went right" and what "went wrong" in your child's prior educational setting. You were probably able to determine if your child's current school is the right fit, or if he or she needs to find an alternative placement. With a better understanding of your child's needs, you can begin looking at some of the important factors that will contribute to success in school. For instance, is the college too big or too small for your child? Are the academics in line with my child's needs? Does the school have the appropriate amount of academic and mental health resources?

Large universities can be overwhelming to individuals, particularly those who are struggling with anxiety and depression. Finding classes, parking, and a peer group can be daunting. Class sizes can also be quite large, and individual help may be difficult to obtain. Alternatively, larger colleges and universities often have a wide variety and timing of classes and majors, including majors that are not as popular. Large schools often also have different social group activities, clubs, and sporting opportunities that may not be available at a smaller school.

Other issues to consider are academics and how rigorous and competitive of a program your child needs to be successful in long-term goals. For instance, if you child is pre-med, is your child's current school a competitive school for this major, and does it have a good track record for successfully getting students in medical schools? Has your child chosen a career in business and wants to pursue a post-graduate MBA? Alternatively, your child could be interested in computer sciences and hopes to get a good paying job with their undergraduate degree. If so, does this school provide the academic support and after college know-how to help them achieve their goals?

Another factor to consider would be culture and environment. Is the school in the city or in a small town? Does your child want a strong sports or fraternity influence? What about weather? Is it too hot, too cold, too much snow, or not enough sunlight? Getting your child to reflect and describe what the most important college attributes are to them will help us hone in on an academic setting they will flourish in.

Also, as discussed in Chapter 6, the availability of academic and mental health support at your child's current or newly chosen academic school will need to be assessed and incorporated into the collaborative treatment plan. Having information about the needed documentation from the academic center before they transition back will help to establish and ensure accommodations are put in place. Here is an example of the academic collaborative treatment plans for an eighteen-year old student, Katie.

Katie

Katie returned from a mid-sized college in the Pacific Northwest after completing her freshman year. Her mom contacted me because her daughter was struggling with depression and struggled to complete her second semester.

Katie expressed a wish to transfer colleges the upcoming year and move closer to home. Her parents were hoping to convince Katie to stay in her current school – she did well academically, and the school had "a great reputation." Katie did not find the school environment was the right "fit for her." She was not able to make any friends in school and felt the culture of the school was "wrong for her." Her college was located in a large urban area, and Katie preferred more outdoor activities, such as hiking and mountain biking. Katie also had a history of learning issues, including ADHD, and did not feel the academic accommodations were sufficient to meet her needs. She stated she spent all her time studying and had no time to eat well, exercise, or socialize. She had a history of social anxiety dating back to middle school and was in and out of therapy for several years.

During Katie's educational autopsy, she consistently expressed her desire to transfer to a larger university close to home. She was able to articulate her reasons to her parents about why she wanted to attend the large university. She felt a large university would be able to provide her with more classes in her desired area of study. She liked the variety of sporting events, interest groups, and social programs, and already knew several students attending this university. She also felt more comfortable being closer to home and being closer to her mental health treatment team. She wanted to continue the progress she was making in therapy. Katie had significant ADHD and wanted to proactively obtain additional accommodations from her new university.

Katie and her parents contacted the student support centers and discovered she would need additional evaluation and documentation of her disabilities. She therefore underwent neuropsychological testing by a local neuropsychologist and was found to have ADHD inattentive type and a learning disorder in the area of mathematics. This information was provided to the university, and accommodations were requested based on these needs. Her transition plan back to college included:

1. Establishing a continued weekly therapy session with her current therapist
2. Submitting accommodation forms and getting her requests approved prior to starting at the university

   - Accommodations requested will include a reduced course load for the first year with full-time status, flexibility with due dates and deadline, a private dorm room, time and half on tests, and a math tutor

3. Meeting with an academic advisor twice during the first semester to monitor progress and assess academic needs
4. Choosing one group or social club to join upon return to the university
5. Attending the orientation week prior to school starting
6. Obtaining her class schedule and putting in place a structured daily routine that incorporates classes, exercise, downtime and sleep
7. Acquiring a referral for a learning specialist who can help her organize her assignments and work on learning skills to help address ADHD and math learning issues

8. Undergoing an evaluation that would assess whether she needs medications to help her focus and concentrate in school or complete assignments or tests in a timely fashion

9. Establishing a crisis plan specific to her school location so that she would know who she can talk with and what numbers to call if she needs additional help or support

10

STEP 7:

Communication, Independence, and Letting Go

As your child is completing the six steps as outlined in the previous chapters, you should start to feel a sense of accomplishment and relief. Your child's depression is improving and he or she developed a solid transition plan back to college. You should be happy with your child's progress, but you might still have underlying fears and concerns about your child. You might be terrified that something will happen to your child when you are not around. How can you ever be okay sending them back? Who will make sure he does well away from home? Who is looking after her? These feelings are normal and working with your own mental health provider may be helpful to address these underlying fears.

I had parents suffer acute stress reactions and even post-traumatic stress-like symptoms in relation to almost losing their child to depression or a suicide attempt while at college. These parents are scared to death to ever let go of their kids, and that is completely understandable. Parents can often bring their own anxieties and other mental health issues into the treatment of their child, which may also need to be identified and addressed.

Common anxieties, such as worries that something bad will happen to your child when you are not there to monitor and protect them and sadness that the parent is no longer "needed," are common feelings when a child leaves for college. These feelings are then compounded when a child is struggling with depression and unable to function at school, leading to worsening fears and anxiety.

Another area of concern comes with the idea that your child technically does not need your permission to take medications, engage in any kind of treatment, or even return to school. This loss of control and allowing your child independence is another big source of fear that comes up for parents.

Communication can also be a major stumbling block for both parents and their kids, and the interaction style between them may be different and should be respected. Learning new ways to communicate with your child now that he is an adult and improving openness, especially around mental health issues, is important. Remaining nonjudgmental and allowing your child the space he or she needs to grow as an individual will improve your child's willingness to talk to you and ask for help and support when needed.

In my own practice, I will often have meetings with parents and the student. If the student allows it, we discuss treatment, progress, school choices, and communication around mental health needs. During this time, I will be assessing if there are any parent-child relationship issues that could be interfering with progress. A big red flag is when a young adult does not want to allow their parents to participate at all in their treatment. When this happens, I will focus more on understanding why this is and work on repairing or building a healthier relationship between child and parents. Some parental issues that can come up and impact your child's treatment and successful transition to college include the parent's own mental health issues and anxiety, poor boundaries (helicopter parent) or being completely uninvolved, a lack of respect for the child's own future goals and wishes, being overly critical or not critical enough (child can do no wrong), feeling uncomfortable with talking about difficult things, or being ashamed of your child's life choices or sexual orientation. I will illustrate some parent-child dynamic issues that can come up utilizing three patient examples.

Megan

As you will recall from Chapter 5, Megan is the nineteen-year-old female with severe depression who left school due to depression and suicidal ideation. Megan's mom was successfully treated for breast cancer, but her path to recovery was hard on the whole family. Megan was often the caretaker for her mom, both physically and emotionally. Megan's own mental health issues typically went unnoticed, and she would often not express her own issues of depression to not worry or burden her mom or dad. She often suffered in silence with no true support system of her own.

Additionally, during her mom's cancer treatment, Megan's mom radically changed the diet of her family, and they were all placed on a strict vegan diet with no processed food allowed in the home. Megan's mom was very critical and controlling of anything that was not perceived to be healthy, including Megan's weight, exercise routine, and friendships. Megan perceived her mom's criticism as proof that she was not good enough and would never be "perfect." She would often not discuss any of her emotional health needs or any of her future goals and desires for fear of criticism.

During initial meetings with Megan and her parents, there was considerable tension in the room. Megan's mom did most of the talking, while Megan's father sat quietly listening, and Megan appeared shut down and distant. She would answer questions minimally and would often not share much about herself when her parents were in the room. However, individually, Megan was very open, cooperative, and engaged. She was clearly depressed, but underneath, there was also a sense of anger and resentment toward her parents that was related to her role as a caretaker and feeling like she was not allowed to be herself without criticism.

On meeting with her parents, we discussed the impact the caretaker role had on Megan. We re-established boundaries by having mom seek support from her husband, friends, or her own therapist, and thereby freeing Megan to work on her new role as an adult and student. Megan's dad was also asked to participate in supporting Megan more and being more involved in her care to strengthen that relationship. Megan's mom was referred to her own mental health providers to address her own depression and anxiety issues and to manage her own fears about health, cancer reoccurrence, perfectionism, etc. We also discussed the impact of Mom's health fears and her need for "perfect health" on Megan. They were perceived as criticism by Megan and resulted in her shutting down, acting out by eating unhealthy foods, and not communicating her own desires and wishes.

Over time, these interventions resulted in improved relation-ships between Megan and her parents. Megan slowly was more open with her own needs and desires and was able to begin sharing her life goals and desires with her parents. When Megan left for school, she was able to communicate effectively with her parents and speak up for herself whenever she needed support.

Joe

In Chapter 8, we met Joe, a nineteen-year-old Latin American male who was the first-born son of highly successful Latin immigrant parents. Both parents brought a different cultural perspective to raising Joe than is typical of current American families, and both parents had a strong investment in ensuring Joe succeed in life. Their primary focus was on pushing Joe to build his "college resume," and Joe's personal and social needs and desires were not considered of major importance. Both parents had a strong sense of what a man should be and were not as familiar with depression – neither parent had any experience with this, and culturally, it was considered a weakness in character.

During our sessions, both parents were invested and present in all meetings and typically made the decisions regarding Joe's care. Joe was often quiet during parent sessions and very agreeable to "whatever" his parents felt was best. Joe was ashamed and embarrassed to talk about his depression and felt judged by his parents for being weak-minded. His parents would often request private therapy sessions to talk about Joe's treatment "without Joe." His parents' appearance of not respecting Joe's input in his own treatment caused Joe to shut down even more.

Early on, boundaries were put in place with Joe's parents to ensure Joe was an active participant in all of his care. I explained to his parents how their overinvolvement in Joe's care was similar to their overinvolvement in his academics during high school. We discussed how Joe did not have his own "voice" and that their desire to have a strong and competent young man was being undermined by their overinvolvement. I indicated that I would only meet with them on occasion and only in the presence of Joe, unless there was an urgent issue. I made Joe update his parents on his mental health treatment. Initially, I was there during the updates for support; but over time, Joe became more independent in relaying the updates to his parents.

Joe was eventually able to teach his parents more about depression, what it is, and how it affected him. His ability to openly talk about his depression and "teach" his parents about it was a major breakthrough for them. Joe's parents were able to have a better understanding of depression overall and how it impacted Joe's ability to do homework, attend class, hang out with friends, or take care of himself. They no longer considered him lazy, not smart enough, or socially "off." His parents recognized their role in preventing open communication and independence and were able to take a less critical and more understanding and empathetic stance.

By teaching his parents about depression, Joe was able to take charge and ownership of his treatment, learn to talk with his parents about his feelings in general, and pave the way for open communication about other life issues. Joe felt more respected by his parents and felt they were now able to "hear him" and know him for the first time. Prior to returning to college, Joe had a great relationship with his parents and was able to ask for support when he needed it. He now stands up for his own ideas, dreams, and life-long goals without fear of criticism.

Katie

As you'll recall from the previous chapter, Katie is the eighteen-year-old female who returned home from college after completing her freshman year. Katie was struggling with depression and had a history of ADHD and immaturity. She expressed a wish to transfer colleges for the upcoming year and move closer to home, but her parents wanted her to stay in her current school since she was doing well academically, and they did not want her to give up so easily.

Her parents were concerned Katie wanted to be closer to home to continue to utilize them for emotional and social support. Katie struggled with separation from her parents most of her life and relied on them "for everything." Katie's mom expressed exhaustion over her daughter's constant emotional needs. Katie struggled socially and often had difficulty making and keeping friends. Her parents were frustrated by her decision to return home as they felt she would never "launch" into being a successful adult if she continued to rely on them so heavily.

I worked with her parents to help them realize that her moving closer to home was not a setback. We discussed Katie's delays in development/maturity and how sending her far away with no safety net from her parents was too overwhelming for her right now. I did support Katie returning to college close by home, but Katie was informed that she would have to live on campus and in a dorm.

Work with Katie and her parents centered, again, around establishing boundaries. This time, the boundaries were more for Katie than her parents. Katie was to only call her parents three times a week at school and could only come home once a month for dinner unless there was a holiday. We built in other support for Katie that included a therapist, psychiatrist, and mentors at school who she was to discuss emotional needs with and gain support from.

By eliminating the need to discuss only her emotional needs with her parents, Katie learned a different way to communicate with her parents that was less one-sided and more equal and reciprocal. Katie and her parents learned to talk about other interests in their lives with each other, and Katie was able to learn more about her parents and who they are. Katie was encouraged and supported to make her own decisions, and her parents were able to feel confident in the decisions that she was making for herself.

Parents often have significant anxiety when their child is not doing well and taking time to assess this in yourself and get the treatment you may need is an important first step. Additionally, identifying and correcting parent-child relationship dynamics will help improve communication, promote independence, and lead to improved outcomes overall. As a parent, having open communication and trust in your child's decisions, and allowing them to grow as independent adults will bring you immeasurable peace of mind. You will be able to breathe, let go, and know your child will become the successful and amazing person they already are.

11

Common Obstacles to Treatment and Transitioning to College

Completing the seven steps in this book should yield a success story for you and your child. Unfortunately, there are some obstacles that could prevent treatment success and or interfere with the transition back to college. We discussed the impact of parent and child dynamics that could pose potential obstacles to care, but there are many more. Some obstacles include difficulties finding the right mental health professionals for you and your child or knowing where to start. Additionally, heavy substance abuse issues, poor motivation, or lack of desire to be in treatment can detrimentally affect care. It is important to address these obstacles early on and look out for potential warning signs to prevent wasted time, money, and treatments.

Finding the Right Treatment Team

This can be one of the most difficult obstacles you will face when looking for help for your child. There is a relative shortage of psychiatrists, psychologists, and social workers available to meet the needs of the general population. Furthermore, there may be a limited number of providers who will be in-network for your insurance plan if that is something that you plan to utilize.

First, start off by asking your child's pediatrician or any family and friends who went through a similar issue for recommendations. You can contact your insurance company and get a list of providers in your insurance network and start there as well. Look for individuals trained specifically in child and adolescent treatment. Given the transition from adolescence to adulthood, they need to have experience with developmental disorders and have systems-based knowledge in the area of family work and schooling.

That being said, there are some adult-trained mental health professionals whose area of focus is young adults, and these individuals are often in collegiate settings. Make sure to ask for a free five- to ten-minute phone consultation to make sure you can talk with the provider about your child's particular issues and ask key questions:

- Are you licensed?
- What are your areas of expertise?
- Do you have expertise working with young adults or adolescents?
- What type of treatment modalities do you use for assessing and treating depression, including medications, types of therapies, supplements, etc.?
- How do you work with the young adult and his or her parents to ensure open communication and treatment updates?
- Are you able to do family therapy or parenting work?
- How do you collaborate with other providers on the

treatment team?

- Are you able to be the leader of the team and help coordinate overall care?
- Did you work with clients struggling in college?
- How do you assist in coordinating the transition back into college?

Before we go into specifics of who you will need on your treatment team, let's review a few key definitions of the various providers available who you will consider being on your child's treatment team.

Psychiatrist

A psychiatrist is a medical physician who is trained in the biological, psychological, and social aspects of mental illness. Typically, their main form of treatment is biological in nature and includes diagnosis, medication evaluations, evaluation for Transcranial Magnetic Stimulation, and other biologically based treatment modalities. Some psychiatrists will also perform therapy as well, but you will typically only find this in private offices where the psychiatrist has more control over the services he or she can provide.

Larger medial groups, hospitals, and community centers primarily utilize psychiatrists as the overall overseer of care and will perform diagnosis and medication evaluations but will then refer to the therapist or other providers within their group. All psychiatrists start out by receiving training in adult psychiatry. Additional training, or what is referred to as fellowship training, is available in several additional areas including child and adolescent psychiatry, addiction psychiatry, forensic psychiatry, and geriatric psychiatry.

Therapist

Therapists are typically either psychologists or social workers who have a clinical license to diagnosis mental health issues and provide therapy. Psychologists have a PhD or PsyD, and social workers have a master's degree to provide clinical care. The training is primarily focused in therapeutic modalities. It is important to ask questions about their treatment modalities and expertise when deciding if this is the right therapist for your child. Psychologists tend to have areas of expertise in certain patient populations due to intensive research or clinical practice training. On the flip side, social workers have additional training in systems issues and coordination of care that can also be quite useful. There are therapists who specifically do family work, individual work, marital counseling, group therapy, and social skills groups and training.

Both types of therapists can be found in large hospitals, community clinics, and in private practice. Most therapists are able to see a wide variety of people and utilize multiple therapeutic strategies to address your needs. However, some therapists can be experts or specialize in certain areas like adolescents, young adults, or substance abuse.

Neuropsychologist

A neuropsychologist is a specially trained psychologist who has expertise in evaluating the impact of brain-based disorders on moods, behaviors, and cognition. Neuropsychologists are often contacted when there is a concern for cognitive issues like learning issues, attention issues, or problems with executive functioning. Neuropsychologists can utilize different types of testing to assess overall IQ; academic achievement; and ability of an individual to focus, think, and learn. Typically, their evaluation is instrumental in making sure the appropriate accommodations are asked for and are met by academic centers.

Nurse Practitioner

Nurse practitioners are advance practice registered nurses, and they can have additional training in the field of psychiatry. Depending on the state, nurse practitioners can work independently or may have to work under a psychiatrist. A nurse practitioner's scope of practice is similar to a psychiatrist in terms of diagnosing and treating with biological treatments such as medications. Unless the nurse practitioner has an additional degree in social work or psychology, most do not perform therapy of any kind.

The choice of which professional to start off with really depends on the severity of the depression, need for medication, types of interventions you feel your child will need, and the type of support he will need to transition back to school.

Speaking with your child's pediatrician would be a good place to start to help identify the most appropriate referral for you. If your child is struggling with moderate to severe depression, then starting with a psychiatrist makes sense. If your child has mild to moderate depression, then finding a local therapist first would be appropriate. If the therapist sees your child as needing more assistance, then a referral can be made at that time. Also, when you talk with the providers beforehand, you can give them a thumbnail version of what is going on, and they should be able to let you know if another type of provider would be needed or necessary prior to your appointment with them.

My best advice is to try and talk with the provider first before the initial appointment to avoid wasting time, money, and frustration of meeting multiple providers who are not the right fit for your child. I would also recommend limiting the number of team members and making sure there is one provider who is the central or overarching coordinator of the treatment. Ideally, you will be able to find one mental health professional to address all of your child's needs, but this is not always possible as the severity and complexity of the issues increases. The most important point here is to make sure that all members of the team talk to each other and have a history of collaborating well.

Poor Motivation

One of the things I hear a lot from parents are frustration statements like, "He won't get out of bed," "She won't even try to exercise," "He is watching YouTube all day," or, "She won't even try to help herself." I often have to discuss how depression can and will hinder the motivation centers in the brain, and it can take a while for their child to recover. Depression can also rob your child of restorative sleep. Even if it looks like your child is getting plenty of it, it can lead to him or her feeling tired and exhausted all day.

I stress patience and understanding during treatment. Nagging and getting "you are being lazy" signals from parents often leads to worsening feelings of shame, guilt, inadequacy, etc. and can lead to your child shutting down even further. Your child already knows that he is not doing much, but I can assure you that he is doing the best that he can do *right now*. Give him the time and space he needs to heal.

If you think about depression as a brain injury, as I often do, you would not expect your child to get better right away. If you look at the brain functioning of individuals struggling with depression, you will see clear differences in activity level and glucose metabolism, pointing to clear brain dysfunction in depression. In order to drive this point home in another way, I use the example of, "If your child blew out his knee, would you expect him to start running a week or two later?" Rest and recovery are needed, and the duration of this time is different for each child and based on the severity of the depression. Acknowledge any progress your child makes and accept that this is your child's journey back.

Know there are times when your child may need some prompting to get moving and start participating more in treatment. If and when this is the case, it should be a member of his treatment team that does the prompting. One of the things I tell parents often is, "Let me be the bad guy." I feel it is the job of your providers to help your child push through his depression, resistance, or whatever is causing him to remain stuck in treatment. Your job is to love your child no matter what and be a source of unconditional support.

Unwillingness to Engage in Treatment or Noncompliance with Treatment

A refusal to engage in care at all or refusal to follow through with any treatment recommendations can be a hard obstacle to navigate. This can look like outright refusal to see any health professional at all, or it can look more like refusal to talk or engage in treatment with the provider. If your child refuses to see anyone for treatment, I would encourage you to start the process and start seeing a mental health provider yourself. Start working through some of the issues discussed in steps one through seven. In working with a therapist, you may be able to identify areas that might be causing your child to have such resistance to treatment and can look at ways to remedy this.

Common reasons for individuals to refuse treatment are mistrust of mental health professionals, feeling ashamed for needing help, and/or worry that they will be labeled "crazy." This was the case for a young adult named Bob, who refused to see me or anyone else for almost six months despite severe depression. He grew up in a household where no one talked about feelings, depression was for the "weak," and his father had a history of making disparaging remarks about people with mental health issues and doctors that just "want to drug everyone up." However, when Bob started struggling, his father contacted me to see if I would be able to treat him. After our first session, Bob refused to come back and made similar disparaging remarks towards me during our initial session. Bob's father was distraught about how to help his son and frustrated that he would not engage in treatment. I recommended that Bob's father meet with me for some education around depression, learn the value of expressing emotions, and to explore his own mistrust of mental health professionals, which stemmed from a past trauma. As Bob's father and I worked together, Bob saw a change in his father's perception of depression and mental health treatment. Bob saw the man he looked up to and respected acknowledge and accept his son's depression, and after six months, Bob engaged in treatment.

If your son or daughter is willing to go to treatment but refuses to engage in treatment recommendations, then that is usually an indication that you are not meeting them where they are or addressing what they consider as most important. In this case, it is important to do more probing of what your child wants. What is your child most worried about? What treatments is your child most concerned about? Does your child want to hear about other modalities of care, such as yoga, acupuncture, herbs, etc.? If your child doesn't want help with depression, is there something else he might need some help with?

I ran into several situations in which parents consider depression to be the number one problem, but their child feels differently. Your child may express only sleep difficulties and feel this issue should be a treatment priority more so than their depression. By initially focusing on your child's identified problem, they are more likely to engage in treatment for sleep and, will feel heard and respected. After sleep is successfully treated, your child may find their depression has improved as well or may be more likely to talk about other treatment options for their depression.

I also work with young adults who do not want any type of traditional treatments and will only consider alternative treatments. The key here is collaboration and working with the child to come up with the best strategy for resolution of the depression, utilizing the most studied alternative strategies and getting them back on track to succeed in whatever healing modality they are most comfortable with.

Most young adults want a say in their care and are more aware of the different complementary and alternative options to treatment. Being open and accepting of their independence in choosing their treatment builds trust and is a key to establishing a long-term therapeutic relationship.

Substance Abuse Issues

The presence of significant substance abuse can greatly impact care, particularly if your son or daughter is unwilling to change his or her substance use behavior. Drugs and alcohol rob your child of the ability to see the impact that substances have on their brains and on their behavior. Brain patterns change and the only thing they can see clearly is how to obtain the next fix. Depression treatment alone is not possible for individuals with moderate to severe addiction issues. Their substance abuse worsens depression by making biological treatments useless, causing neurochemical changes in the brain to keep them depressed, and it destroys relationships. For moderate to severe substance abuse issues, either a detox or rehab program is likely necessary. Additionally, finding experts in the area of substance abuse counseling is needed to get your child's substance abuse treatment started immediately. Parents can also reach out to organizations that help families, such as Al-Anon, learn to cope with the challenges of addiction issues.

In this chapter, we explored some additional obstacles that can impact your ability to find the care your child needs to get his depression treated and back in college. As noted, it is important to address these obstacles early on to avoid wasted time and money on ineffective treatment. The cost of inadequate or ineffective care is immeasurable, and although patience is important during this process, an urgency to resolve the depression is not. Finding the right treatment team is critical to make sure steps one through seven are accomplished and successful. Finding the right treatment professionals to evaluate the issues and avoid the obstacles in this chapter will make the treatment process smooth for both you and your child.

You can do this, Mom and Dad! You have the tools in this book to make sure your child is getting the best assessment available. You have a step-by-step process to ensure you have selected the appropriate academic placement for your child. You established trust, boundaries, and worked on effective communication with your child. Your anxiety, fears, and worries should be easing by now, and soon you will launch your child off into adulthood knowing he will succeed.

12

You Got This, Mom and Dad

Remember Linda from the beginning of the book? She was the forty-eight-year-old married mother who got a call from her son's school that he was sent to the ER and hospitalized for depression and suicidal ideation. She had to go pick her son up from a hospital in another state and bring him home only to struggle with figuring out how to find the right help her son needed to treat his depression and get him back into school. You may recall that Linda and her husband were scared, confused, frustrated, and feeling a sense of shame and hopelessness.

After Linda contacted me, I worked through the seven steps of this book with her, her husband, and her son Tom over the course of a year to help her son get his depression treated and safely transition back into college. I walked them through the seven steps as described in this book. In the first step, we assessed the origins of Tom's depressive symptoms, and from there we moved on to step two, which explored many different mainstream and complementary approaches for treatment.

Tom's treatment options were selected based on severity of his symptoms and in collaboration with his choices of desired treatments. I discussed the concept of an integrative treatment approach with Tom and his parents, and we explored other complementary techniques for Tom, including meditation and herbal supplements. Tom and his parents were also introduced to the importance of diet, exercise, and sleep for depression treatment and overall wellness, and an assessment of needs in these areas was performed.

In step three, we performed an education autopsy of Tom's current college to determine what worked and what did not work for him in college. Based on this autopsy, we decided a change in college environment would be our next best step for him.

Step four was then initiated to explore specific developmental factors that were contributing to Tom's depression and problems in college. The information from step one through four was then gathered, and in step five, we developed a holistic and collaborative treatment plan for Tom's depression. This plan was developed as an integrative treatment plan that was patient-centered and in-line with Toms desired treatment wishes and goals. Tom's plan also incorporated dietary changes, exercise regimens, and sleep hygiene skills that were important during treatment and also as part of a life-long wellness program to improve mind-body health and resiliency from future mental health issues.

Similarly, in step six, we pulled information from steps one through four to find an appropriate college for Tom. He selected a smaller school closer to home that had excellent academic and mental health services on campus. Additionally, Tom was able to apply for and obtain accommodations based on his mental health needs to ease back into school and reduce the stress of his transition.

Finally, in step seven, I addressed issues of changing parenting roles with Tom's parents. This step occurred throughout treatment and focused on building boundaries, openness, and collaboration. We also addressed underlying issues of parental anxiety in both of Tom's parents until they were confident that their child was safe, happy, and ready to move forward as an adult and head back to college.

Ultimately, Tom was able to heal fully from his depression, transition back to a new school, and graduate several years later with a degree in engineering. He no longer struggles with episodes of depression. He continues to utilize the coping strategies he learned in treatment and kept up with his meditation, exercise, and diet routines.

Young adults do get better, and depression and dropping out of college are not failures. I view them as opportunities to learn and change the direction of one's life in a positive way. Tom was clearly struggling before, and his depression presented an opportunity to assess and address issues that caused his depressive symptoms. I believe utilizing the seven steps made a big difference in Tom's treatment, and so does Linda.

After completing treatment, Linda and her husband no longer felt scared or overwhelmed by the thought of their son harming himself, not finishing college, or being depressed "forever." Linda knew her son had the resources and skills he needed to be successful. She also knew that both she and her son could find treatment in the future if he needed it. Linda and her husband were both able to establish an open-door communication policy with their son that was appropriate and established and maintained boundaries that felt good to everyone. Linda addressed her own anxieties and concerns and now feels confident that her son is safe, happy and healthy.

Thank You

Thank you so much for reading *My Child's Not Depressed Anymore*. I know that you are now armed with the information you need to get your son or daughter the care they need to eliminate depression. You also now have the information to navigate the collegiate systems and get your child back in school.

I would love to learn more about your journey and success in getting your child back on track. Please keep in touch on my newly formed Facebook page and visit www.drlsquared.com for more resources.

About the Author

Dr. Melissa Lopez-Larson is a board-certified psychiatrist for adults, children, and adolescents. She received her MD from the University of Cincinnati School of Medicine. Dr. Lopez-Larson performed her adult and child psychiatry training at Harvard Medical School training sites, including Massachusetts General Hospital, McLean Hospital, and Cambridge Hospital.

For over fifteen years, she practiced in a variety of settings, including academic research, inpatient, residential, and outpatient psychiatric services. She has extensive clinical and research experience and completed an integrative medicine fellowship in the fall of 2017. Through this fellowship, Melissa developed a diverse knowledgebase in complementary mind-body techniques to further personalize her approach to helping patients heal. Her unique skill set resulted in the establishment of a practice in Park City, Utah, that combines classic psychiatric services with evidence-based complementary treatments, supplements, nutrition, meditation and other modalities, including Transcranial Magnetic stimulation (TMS), to provide an individual with a holistic approach to the treatment of mental health related issues.

Melissa lives with her family in Park City. She enjoys spending time with her family traveling to the beach and skiing the best powder on earth. She also enjoys golfing and hiking in the beautiful mountains during the spring and summer.

Website: https://www.drlsquared.com
Email: Melissa@drlsquared.com